Love Codes x

UNDERSTANDING MEN'S SECRET
BODY LANGUAGE

Elayne Kahn
and
David Rudnitsky

GUILD PUBLISHING
LONDON · NEW YORK · SYDNEY · TORONTO

This edition published
1989 by Guild Publishing
by arrangement with
Piatkus Books

CN 9004

Printed in Great Britain

Contents

Introduction

W hen women talk about their disappointments in love, a single refrain is sounded over and over again: 'If only I had known what he was really like *before* I was so deeply involved.' Almost everyone makes the wrong romantic choice at least once in their lives; others repeat the same mistakes many times and discover they never get any less painful.

It doesn't have to be that way. There are techniques for separating the men from the boys, and for identifying the man who is warm, generous and sincere and will give totally in a love relationship. And there are also ways to win him over. *Love Codes* offers women everywhere the tools they need to unlock a man's true romantic nature.

This book is a practical guide to understanding what makes a man tick. It looks at men's personal preferences and patterns of behaviour so that you can identify the partners who are most appropriate for *you*.

Love Codes are everywhere and the key to finding them is knowing where to look. A man displays Love Codes through his body language – in the way he dresses, how he decorates his flat, the hobbies he enjoys, how he responds when irritated or disappointed, and his history of past involvements. You can find Love Codes in his driving, his behaviour at a party, the way he arranges his books on the shelves, and even the position he sleeps in.

By understanding these Love Codes you will be able to

determine whether a man is selfish or generous, open or closed, faithful or deceptive. They allow you to find out his true attitudes towards sex, raising a family, and accepting emotional responsibility. And an accurate reading of his behaviour and the signals he gives out consciously and unconsciously tells you whether he is capable of sustaining a long-term involvement or whether he just wants a short-term affair.

HOW LOVE CODES WORK

But why do Love Codes work at all? Why are they the key to finding out what he's really like? From a psychological point of view, the choices a man makes and the behaviour he exhibits are a way of expressing the many different facets of his personality. To the trained eye, these clues are as unmistakable as fingerprints. And the more you observe about a man, the more able you will be to understand his true nature and choose your involvements more wisely.

Of course, the techniques of observing and deciphering the Love Codes in his day-to-day activities take a bit of practice. And that's why we've written this book. Read the case histories presented here and do the quizzes provided throughout. Look for the clues we discuss in every aspect of his life. Once you have compiled the information you need, use it to assess his eligibility. Don't seek perfection but if you observe an unappealing pattern, don't stick around too long hoping that he will change – or worse, believing that you can change him.

If you like what you see, however, the information you gain from his Love Codes will be doubly useful. Knowing his expectations, prejudices and concerns helps you respond to him with warmth, tenderness and understanding. Compassion for his weaknesses helps you break down his emotional barriers and gain his trust. By understanding the psychological dimensions of a man, you can make an informed judgement about him that is neither totally intellectual nor completely emotional. It is in that climate that a deep and meaningful love relationship can take root and grow.

WHY WE MAKE THE WRONG CHOICES

It all sounds so simple, yet women are notorious for making the wrong choices about the men they get involved with. Why do some of us repeat the same patterns over and over again? One reason is that we look with deliberate blindness at a new man in our life because we are so eager to find a fulfilling relationship. We choose to ignore signals that clearly identify him as unsuitable and we pretend to see the potential for lasting happiness in order to alleviate the present loneliness.

In the long run this strategy doesn't work. The sorrows and satisfactions of a relationship are usually visible from the outset if we allow ourselves to see them. That means not making excuses for your man. How often have you explained away someone's deficiences with any of the following statements:

- 'He doesn't dress well because he isn't making enough money.'
- 'His house is a mess because he lives alone.'
- 'He's afraid of becoming involved because he's still getting over the hurt from his last relationship.'
- 'He doesn't want me to see my friends because he loves me so much he can't bear to be without me.'
- 'He has a drinking problem because he never felt love. But I can restore his faith in humanity.'

Obviously no one is perfect and there are reasonable explanations for some of his failings. The problem arises when a pattern of weakness starts to emerge. Deciphering his Love Codes helps you distinguish between minor quirks that won't endanger a rewarding relationship and serious personality defects that will.

What are some of the other reasons why women make so many mistakes in their choice of partners?

- Many women reach a point in their lives where they feel an overpowering need to be in a relationship, often when their friends pair off or when their biological clock begins to tick loudly. In this state of emotional readiness, a woman may fool herself into believing that any eligible and interested man has the qualities of her ideal mate.
- A strong sexual connection can often mask the reality of a relationship. An intense physical attraction can make both parties feel they have alleviated the loneliness and isolation that are so much a part of the human condition. A woman may hold fast to her fantasy that she has found the perfect companion because letting go of that myth means taking the risk of being alone again.
- She selects someone who appears – on an intellectual plane – to have all the attributes of an 'appropriate' husband. Perhaps he is good-looking and considered desirable by many other women. Or, he may be financially secure, socially well-connected, or tied to a fast-paced crowd that will make her life more exciting. Choosing a man by his list of credentials, rather than by the emotional intimacy you can achieve, is a certain way to be disappointed.
- Because the man she is interested in appears easygoing and accommodating, she mistakenly believes that she will be able to change him. What she fails to realise is that many men, like many women, are most flexible in the early stages of a relationship, when they are trying to impress you. But as he grows more comfortable, his true personality will emerge. A relationship in which either party hopes to remake the other is doomed.

To find true happiness, you have to break the destructive habits of your past and cast a more objective eye on the men you meet. *Love Codes* will help you do just that.

THE SIX KEY QUESTIONS

Six all-important questions must be answered before you become seriously involved with a new love partner. Accurate answers to these questions are based on a careful scrutiny of his Love Codes.

1. He makes a great first impression, but is it for real?

We all try to put our best foot forward, and in the courting stage a man is likely to treat you with kindness and generosity. If he is aware of his failings, he may try hard to cover them up, but in time the truth is sure to emerge. The man who appears decisive may actually be unsure and insecure, and the one who seems submissive may really be an expert manipulator.

Certain men, in fact, are quite adept at putting on an act intended to charm – or disarm – you. But during his unguarded moments – and we will point out exactly when those occur – his Love Codes let you see the truth for yourself. Had you observed, for example, how he tips, shakes hands or crosses the street, you might have anticipated that this man's sizzle would soon fizzle.

2. Does he really want a relationship?

The only thing that terrifies some men more than intimacy is showing how much they fear it. Many women complain about men who have appeared genuinely interested in them, only to back off when the relationship takes a more serious turn. Suddenly he stops calling, starts arguments or makes unreasonable demands.

How do you know whether he's looking for a long-term involvement? Analyse his Love Codes! Read on to learn what his past relationships, his job history and his household furnishings reveal about his willingness to make a commitment.

3. What kind of a sexual partner will he be?

In order to be an exciting, yet sensitive lover, a man must be sensual, open and as concerned about your needs as he is about his own. The man who knows that both partners must be satisfied in order for sex to be meaningful is concerned about bringing warmth to the bedroom and making you feel safe and secure there.

How can you discern his sexual responses before you go to bed together? Analyse his Love Codes! Find out how you can tell whether your man is sexually liberated by the food he loves, the photographs in his home and his abilities on the dance floor.

4. Will he be emotionally supportive?

A desirable love match will contribute to your personal success, rather than hinder it. Such a man believes your goals are as important as his and he seeks a healthy and independent relationship, not an emotionally crippling one. Nurturing and supportive men thrive on the emotional growth of the women closest to them.

How do you know whether he will provide the emotional support you need? Analyse his Love Codes! There is much to be learned by noticing who determines the evening's itinerary, whether he asks about your preferences and how he responds when you seek advice.

5. What is he really looking for in a woman?

Fearful of rejection, men often tell women just what they want to hear, not what they really mean. Perhaps he professes to admire independent women, but eventually you discover that he prefers someone who fits traditional role models. Or he tells you he wants to settle down but changes the subject each time the issue of commitment arises. If the truth emerges once you feel emotionally attached, it can be particularly shattering.

How do you know what is important to him in a relationship? Analyse his Love Codes! A peek into his wardrobe or medicine cabinet, a glance at his jewellery, a thought about his kisses reveal volumes of information. His personal mementos tell you much about his values and the types of associations he values in life.

6. Will he eventually hurt me?

Little in life is more painful than the collapse of a relationship in which you placed great hopes. Although we must take risks in our emotional lives if we are to reap the rewards of interpersonal involvement, women also must protect themselves by understanding a man's psyche before getting deeply involved with him. Too often we are unrealistic or blind to his signals simply because we see only what we want to see.

How do you know whether you are in for emotional heartbreak? Analyse his Love Codes! Fastidious neatness, sleeping with clenched fists and a preference for pastel colours reveal hidden messages that are important for women to understand as they embark on the adventure of a new involvement.

Love Codes, then, gives you all the information you need to make the critical choices about your romantic involvements.

By teaching you to think with your head *and* your heart, Love Codes are the intelligent way to approach your most intimate attachments. Read on and find out how you can spark the magic of romance in an atmosphere of mutual admiration and genuine understanding.

1

Something in the way he moves

What does it mean when he folds his arms over his chest while you speak? Why are his eyes darting around the room instead of looking at you? Why does he always walk so slowly that you have to stop to let him catch up?

Love Codes aplenty lurk behind a man's body language and his physical preferences. Many of them are unconsciously adopted, longstanding habits of which he is only dimly aware; others change to reflect his mood and alert you to the moments when he feels insecure. From the way he sits and stands, to how he shakes hands and whether he makes eye contact while talking to you, careful observations give you great insight *before* you get too deeply involved.

Look for the man whose physical messages convey assurance, not arrogance – he knows what he wants in life and love and is emotionally mature enough to give of himself to others. Caution is called for when a man's Love Codes suggest that he lacks confidence in himself; he who bumbles along in life may also bumble along in love. Although such a man may be loyal and emotionally committed, you will have to put a lot of effort into bolstering his confidence. Steer clear when his Love Codes translate as self-centred or domineering.

HOW HE SITS TELLS YOU WHERE HE STANDS

When you first sit down to chat with a man, check his posture; notice the position of his hands and legs, observe how he moves his head, and pay attention to how close he sits to you. His sitting position at the beginning of a conversation, and the way that it changes throughout your discussion, provide a surprisingly accurate gauge to his feelings and his interest in romance.

DONALD: LEANING TOWARDS A RELATIONSHIP

Emma: *I met Donald at a party and really enjoyed talking to him. He was bright, witty and attentive, and we talked easily together. He described his successful management consulting business to me in confident, but not boastful, terms. But he sat at a distance that made conversation awkward, forcing me to lean unnaturally towards him to hear what he was saying. He looked directly at me while talking, but I noticed that he kept his legs crossed and angled away from me.*

In their earliest meeting, Donald gave Emma several important clues about himself. His wit, intelligence and attentiveness comprised a menu seductive enough to arouse Emma's interest. And, by focusing directly at Emma, Donald revealed his genuine interest in her.

Certain Love Codes, however, suggest that caution may be in order before becoming too hopeful that he will be the new man in her life. Despite his success in business and his intellectual confidence, Donald is clearly fearful of a relationship. His crossed legs, guarding his most sensitive organs, suggest that he's concerned about being hurt emotionally. What's more, by positioning himself in such a way that Emma has to lean towards him, he reveals a need to remain in control.

Here, then, is a man who desires intimacy but is afraid of it. The question that remains to be answered is how long it will take Donald to feel secure enough with a woman to open up.

Emma: *We talked for almost an hour about everything under the sun – books, politics, theatre, you name it. We shared quite a lot in common and I could tell that he was beginning to relax with me. He finally uncrossed his legs, leaned closer in my direction, and pulled his chair in so tight that his knees were almost touching mine.*

Initially, Donald distanced himself from Emma, but as he grew more comfortable with her, he uncrossed his legs, a gesture symbolising candour. Drawing his chair closer to her was also an affirmative sign, indicating that he is willing to compromise when it seems appropriate and doesn't always have to maintain tight control over a situation.

All in all, Donald looks like a good risk. His initial defensiveness was eventually supplanted with an openness as he shed the emotional barriers that he had first erected.

Other sitting positions

Reclining with his legs stretched out

Although his posture appears laid-back and relaxed, the man who sits for long periods in this position is actually exerting a subtle form of control by forcing you to sit at his level in order to communicate. Although he is not out-wardly aggressive, he has a stubborn streak and may listen politely to your opinions, but will then go ahead and do things his own way.

On the edge of his seat

A man who always sits as though he is ready to take off is loaded with nervous energy and enthusiastic about trying new things. He propels himself at full force into relationships, throwing all caution to the wind, but is impatient if things don't move along quickly. At least he's not shy, though, and won't hesitate to ask for your phone number as soon as you meet. His freneticism will scare some women away; if you prefer to develop relationships at a more leisurely pace, think carefully before agreeing to even a first date.

Both feet on the ground

Here is a levelheaded man who is genuinely open and relaxed about relating to you. He is not afraid to be a bit vulnerable and the initial signals he sends suggest that he wants to explore at least the possibility of a relationship.

Be alert to the distance between his legs – if he always keeps them just a few inches apart, chances are that he is rather rigid in his thinking and not much of an innovator. But if he moves them a lot, keep an eye on what signals the motions. You know you are striking a responsive chord when his legs swing wide open. And the issue you raise is probably a sensitive one if he closes his legs tightly together.

Hands in his lap

This is a rather dainty position for a man to take. He has obviously learned his manners, probably at the knee of a very domineering mother who drilled him in the importance of good behaviour. Reserved, but tense and conservative to a fault, he is more concerned with saying the right thing than letting you know what is really on his mind. In a relationship he will be the perpetual peacemaker, sometimes at the expense of honesty.

Hands clasped between the knees

This is a clear expression of ambivalence, especially if his legs are crossed at the same time. On guard against invaders, he leaves almost no open space for you to reach. Unless he shifts from this position rather quickly, he is too self-protective to be good relationship material.

Sitting on his hands

This man is struggling to keep his emotions under control, possibly because he is aware of his own tendency towards overly aggressive behaviour. In a relationship, too, he is likely to hold back his displeasure for days or weeks, then suddenly let loose with an outburst of emotion. He is somewhat difficult to deal with, but it isn't hard to learn where his sensitive spots are – and how to avoid touching them.

IS HE UPRIGHT?

You are most likely to meet a man while the two of you are standing up, so this is the ideal time to look for your first clues. Observe how far apart from you he stands, notice his posture, and listen to the signals that reveal the level of his self-confidence or the extent of his anxiety and tension.

DAVID: DON'T FENCE HER IN!

Michelle: *Early in March, I met David at a gallery opening. He was well-dressed, with an appealing air of sophistication about him, and we stood talking together in an uncrowded corner of the room. He leaned close to me, resting his shoulder against the wall, and was obviously quite at ease with himself. I enjoyed talking with him, but I felt a bit isolated because he had positioned himself in such a way that my view of the rest of the party was cut off.*

David's sophistication was certainly a turn-on for Michelle, and his confidence was clearly expressed in his relaxed posture and in his willingness to stand close to her. Unfortunately, his position also signalled a tendency to control the women he becomes involved with. By blatantly encroaching on her space, he was both figuratively and literally boxing her in, a pattern that would undoubtedly continue throughout their relationship.

The messages in other standing positions

Wide open

This position of openness suggests someone who feels neither threatened nor wary of the woman he is talking with. Observe how he holds his arms in this position; if they are at rest by his side, he feels no need to be on guard with you. If they are folded across his chest, however, he has not learned to relax completely. Chances are good, however, that in time he will move towards an even more open stance.

Shifting interest

Sometimes a man shifts his balance from one foot to another merely to relieve the discomfort of standing for a long time. However, if he moves closer to you while leaning on one foot, then further away while leaning on the other, you have a clear indication of his ambivalence. Perhaps you are worthy of further attention, he muses, but then again, perhaps not. Later in a relationship, he will continue to hedge his bets on you, yielding at one moment to the temptation of commitment and then backing away from it at the next.

Rigid backbone

This posture is assumed by a man who is well-disciplined, very successful and incorrigibly set in his ways. Although he cuts an impressive figure, he does not always allow himself to have much fun. But the woman who respects his conservative values and needs a pillar of strength to lean on will find him just the right person to meet her needs.

Jogger

He signals his impatience from the start by letting you know that just as soon as you finish talking he has something important to say. Energetic and able to think on his feet, he doesn't always take the time to reflect fully on things and won't take your needs and opinions into full account. He's energetic, though, and if you don't demand too much personal attention, he can certainly be a lot of fun.

GESTURES SPEAK LOUDER THAN WORDS

A man's hands provide a direct sight line to the thoughts in his head. The motions of the hand are versatile and varied, shifting as mood and comfort levels change, enabling the observant to pick up on his temperamental shifts and to notice how he responds as differing topics of conversation arise.

RICHARD: A GESTURE OF SINCERITY

Diane: *Richard's gestures were the first thing about him to catch my eye. We chatted about a range of rather personal topics, from our jobs to our pending divorces, and I kept noticing how he used expressive hand gestures to emphasise his points. At first, the palms of his hands were outstretched at his side, facing his own body. But as our conversation became more animated, he turned his hands so that the palms were facing me. Later in our conversation, he moved his hands away from his body and closer to me. Throughout our talk, I sensed that he was unusually open and straightforward about his feelings.*

Diane has discovered Richard's essential honesty, which is revealed in part by his open palms. By gradually turning his palms outward, he suggests a willingness to be forthcoming – once he is convinced that you are trustworthy and receptive to him. The emphatic quality of his hand gestures suggests that he is more demonstrative than most men and has not built particularly high walls around himself.

Other hand signals

Hands in pockets

A man who keeps his hands in his pocket is protecting his most vulnerable parts – his genitals – which indicates a tendency to keep his innermost feelings to himself. By the same token, he does not readily reach out and touch other people. You will find that this man needs a lot of assurance before he is willing to make himself more accessible to you.

Hands touching you

A man who brushes you from time to time or touches your arm as he makes his points is forthright and direct in his approach. Clasping your arm as he makes a joke is also a sign of genuine affection and indicates a warm and healthy interest in things physical. It is best to be rather wary, however, if he jabs at you or touches you often enough to make you feel uncomfortable. These signs of hostility belie his pleasant words and suggest that he is harbouring some deep anger.

Clenched fists

A clear sign of exasperation, the man who stands in a crowd with his fists clenched is tense and uncomfortable in most social situations. Move cautiously with this man – in a relationship, he is likely to take all the frustrations of his life out on you.

Flamboyant gestures

Here is a man passionate about his convictions, a little overly dramatic, and so charmingly aggressive that he'll besiege you with flowers and chocolates once he decides to win your heart. Although he can be a bit overpowering at times, and tends to be self-consciously pleased with his powers of showmanship, it is hard to go too wrong with a man who never runs short of praise for your beauty and lets you know in words and deeds that he finds you thoroughly desirable.

Fingers locked together, hands at rest

His motto is 'all things in moderation', and you'll find this man to be patient, reflective, and genuinely interested in what you have to say. Even-tempered and consistent, he thinks carefully about his priorities in life and once he decides that he is interested, he'll pursue you with under-stated determination. He is not particularly receptive to spontaneous ideas and doesn't like to have his plans thwarted, but at least he won't spring unpleasant surprises on you.

IT'S ALL IN THE HANDSHAKE

In many European countries friends and even casual acquaintances greet each other with effusive hugs and kisses on both sides of the cheek. But in this country the handshake is the most socially accepted form of physical contact between two people. We shake hands when we are introduced and again when we depart, after a business deal has been clinched or a personal dispute settled, and when a winner has been declared in a sporting event.

With all their practice, though, men are seldom aware of how much *they* communicate with every shake, which is why you can learn so much by paying attention to it. Keep in mind, however, that men do know how much *another* person's handshake reveals to them. A woman who grips a man's hand warmly and firmly, rather than like a dead fish or with an aggressive vengeance, is a woman likely to attract a man's attention.

JONATHAN: A GRIP ON LIFE

Vanessa: *I noticed Jonathan talking to an old college friend of mine at a party, but he made no particular impression on me. I was enjoying myself dancing, drinking and talking to other friends and we weren't introduced until late in the evening. Finally, though, he came over to introduce himself. I was immediately taken by the warmth and strength conveyed in his handshake. I thought to myself, 'Here is a man who must be warm and strong in other areas of his life, too.'*

The fact that Jonathan's sincere handshake provoked interest from a woman who had previously paid little attention to him is a testimony to its power. A limp hand-shake conveys the feeling of inadequacy, whereas a firm – but not overbearing – shake exudes warmth and confidence. A handshake can disarm someone or turn them off completely.

Other handshake messages

Long squeeze

A seductive and sensual man, he's also assertive enough to seek out what he wants – and hold on to it when he finds it. If you're interested in him, too, why not go for it? One exception though: holding on to your hand for too long is a manipulative tactic, warning you that he expects to be in charge.

Moist palm

He may look calm, cool and collected, but his damp palm gives him away. This man is perpetually nervous but he knows how to suppress it. Perhaps he has learned to suppress other strong emotions, too. It may take a while for this man to relax and trust you, but there is a reservoir of strong feelings running through him.

Limpness

Watch out! The only thing this man is committed to is being weak and indecisive. A man who extends a limp hand to you lacks zest for life and has not learned the art of an equal relationship; he's much more comfortable with his role as victim.

Vicelike grip

A firm shake is one thing, a tight and painful grip quite another. Whether this man has a streak of cruelty about him or is genuinely unaware of his effect on others, his painful clasp should trigger a warning to approach with extreme caution.

Two-hands

A genuine gesture of pleasure at meeting you, the man who covers your hand in the two of his wears his heart on his sleeve and doesn't stand on formality or social convention. He may come on a bit strong, but he is a generous and genuine person who can really be counted on in a relationship. When he falls for someone, he falls for her without any hesitation or reservation.

Pumper

Energetic, assertive and outgoing, you've found a man who stays active around the clock. A born extrovert, he is the hale and hearty type who comes on with enthusiasm. If you have the stamina for him, there's lots of fun in store.

Tickling palm

This is a rather flirtatious gesture that lets you know this man has sexual designs on you. Whether the move seems crude or bold and inviting depends a lot on your own inclination and attraction. Don't expect a meaningful relationship with this man, though; chances are he is more interested in a passing sexual encounter.

GETTING TO KNOW HIM STEP-BY-STEP

Walking is literally body language in motion. The gestures, attitudes and pace in a man's forward stride are often unconscious, and a careful onlooker can spot significant clues about his self-image, how he relates to the environment around him and how interested he really is in his companion.

KEVIN: THE LEADER OF THE PACK

Carol: *It is absolutely impossible to have a conversation when I walk with Kevin. He strides quickly forward, forcing me to lag several paces behind him. And I still feel breathless when we reach our destination. Occasionally he'll stop so that I can catch up with him, but as soon as I do, he is off like a shot again. He laughs about it and calls me a slowcoach, but it makes me mad.*

Carol's irritation stems from her desire for an equal relationship in which both parties travel the path of life together. Kevin, a high achiever unwilling to slow his insistent stride, is not the man to meet that need. Too eager to stay ahead of the competition in his professional life, he just can't slow down in his personal life. Concerned about the implications for other areas of her relationship, Carol

may decide to let Kevin walk away. But if you are attracted to a man driven by vision and determination, you may be willing to walk two paces behind him.

Other walking signals

Slower than the rest

Forcing others to wait is a devious and subtle approach to asserting control, but it is as effective as a speedy pace. The man who has learned how to exert influence from a sub-servient position has an ability to manipulate a love relationship in a way that will always leave you bewildered. Like the speed walker, he can't be counted on to adapt to your needs.

Hunched

Here is a man who has been bent by the burdens of the world and the disappointments in his own life, and he is ready to curl into a protective ball. Although his negative outlook on life can be depressing to a woman with a similar temperament, his unassuming qualities may appeal to a woman weary of arrogant men. You will find that he respects your strength and is very dependent on you.

Looking ahead

Eyes front and centre, here's a man heading relentlessly towards his goals. He's a real go-getter with impressive powers of concentration and he'll brook no distractions. He's an eligible match for a woman of equal determination and drive but be prepared to make a lot of concessions if yours is a more relaxed approach to life.

Looking around

By contrast, this man is never in too much of a hurry to stop and smell the flowers – or stroll through an antique shop, watch a juggler on the street corner or sit on a park bench and watch the world pass by. If you can't tolerate someone who is frequently late and lacks single-minded ambition, pass him by. But if a curious adventurer appeals to you, you've found your man.

Nose in the air

Many men who stride as though they are too important to look down at the plebeians below them are just as aloof and unapproachable as they appear. The truth is that they are more insecure than the average man and find it easier to keep others at a distance than to make the effort to extend themselves. If you are lucky, you may be able to crack that reserved facade and find a warm and caring individual, but not all women will find the effort worth the trouble.

The bopper

This is a man who hears music where none is playing, loves a sunny day and has a word of encouragement and good cheer for everyone he meets. Even at the ripe old age of 50, he'll still have the energy and vitality of an adolescent. There is a spring in his step and a lightness in his approach to the world. His exuberance and playfulness are extra-ordinarily refreshing.

DANCING LOVE CODES

Dancing is an almost universal form of communication, one that transcends cultural and social boundaries. As a dance partner, your man leaves behind clues with every twirl – although it is not difficult to tell a lie, it is very difficult to dance one. His fluidity, or lack of it, hints at his sexuality, tells you whether he can let his hair down for a good time, and warns you if he is repressed or anxious about his feelings. Whether you bop, boogie, free-style or waltz, watch your partner for important personality clues.

MICHAEL: WAS HE LOOKING FOR A DANCING FOOL?

Dorothy: *I was in heaven when we danced together. Michael was so romantic. He held me very close and led me very firmly around the floor. His lips brushed my ear a few times as he whispered compliments about my dancing, my body and my dress. At the end of a dance he bowed to me, kissed my hand and was off in search of a new partner. He danced with many other women at the party.*

As the party was breaking up, Michael approached to say good night and ask for my phone number. I was thrilled to give it to him but bewildered as I watched him leave the house with his arm around one of his other dancing partners.

The confidence Michael conveys on the dance floor is consistent with his smooth and polished manner. In both his personal and professional life, he is a natural leader who likes to be firmly in control. His sensual dancing reveals a desire to share intimate emotional experiences and hints at his strong sexual inclinations.

Beware, however, of a man who behaves romantically

17

towards every dance partner. He may be arousing to dance with but totally uninterested in developing a relationship once the music stops. This is a man who enjoys playing the field and is in no hurry to settle down.

What does his dancing style reveal?

Now, look at the following questions and scrutinise your answers carefully to learn what kind of a lover your dance partner will be.

1. Does he execute the proper steps with such precision that you'd think he is still in dance class?

Here is a man who follows instructions carefully but is too scared to break out of a practiced routine. In a relationship, he acts predictably and according to the rules of proper behaviour but finds it hard to be spontaneous.

2. Is he able to improvise without losing all sense of rhythm?

The ability to improvise suggests a man with a strong sense of self that translates into a charming unpredictability in a romance. Just when you think you understand him, he'll excite you by revealing another twist in his personality. His ability to be flexible is helpful when you are trying to solve problems in your relationship.

3. Are his dance movements fluid and smooth?

Few things are more appealing than a man who exudes grace and confidence on the dance floor. An indication that his emotional and physical selves are harmonious, he is likely to be as strongly sexual in bed as he is sensual on the dance floor.

4. Or are his movements tentative and jerky?

If he looks uncomfortable on the dance floor, he may merely be uneasy in a crowd where he feels that he is being asked to perform. Although he may be sexually unsure, he could just as likely be sensitive and arousing on a one-to-one basis.

5. Does he hold you close or keep you at arm's length?

Few things are more revealing about how a man feels about intimacy than the length at which he holds you while dancing. Someone who holds you close indicates that he is willing to let you into his private space and is eager to touch and hold you. A man who keeps you at a distance says, in essence, that he prefers a degree of independence and won't allow you to occupy too much of his time.

6. Does he lead well?

There is an art to leading well that balances your ability to improvise with the importance of good teamwork on the dance floor. The man who rigidly controls your every move most likely views himself as a strong and protective provider and does not easily let go of stereotypical male roles. By contrast, the leader who gives you room to shine on the dance floor is a man who will also allow you to play a leading role in your relationship.

7. Will he follow you when you know the dance steps and he does not?

A man's willingness to learn from you on the dance floor is certain to carry into other realms of his life. An openness to learn new things and a willingness to admit that he does not know all the answers are keys to a mature and long-lasting relationship.

8. Does he look at you while you are dancing together or do his eyes wander all over the dance floor?

If his eyes are focused on you, it suggests that at least for the moment you are the centre of his universe and he has no interest in becoming involved with anyone else. Beware if his eyes are wandering – he could simply be a voyeur, observing others at a distance, but he may also be looking for another romantic outlet.

9. Is he showing off for others?

The mark of an obsessive performer, he's more concerned with impressing others than relating to you. A show-off usually substitutes the attention of others for his own lack of confidence and often demands so much reassurance that your own needs are neglected.

10. Does he like a variety of dances or does he stick to one familiar step?

A person who likes to dance to a number of different steps is someone with diversified interests and an ongoing curiosity about the world. He will value a relationship built on new discoveries and avoids monotony by experimenting and seeking out new directions. By contrast, the man who dances in one familiar way is scared to break out of the patterns he knows best and you may eventually feel stifled with him.

PETER: UNPOLISHED BUT SMOOTH

Sharon: *Peter lacked almost all the social graces. An awkward conversationalist with a knack for saying the wrong thing at the wrong time, he was not terribly popular with women. But get him on the dance floor and an astonishing transformation took place. No woman in the room could say no when he asked for a dance. He shone there − and there alone − with the confidence and imagination that seemed to be missing in every other realm of his life.*

Awkward in most social situations, Peter has found his forté on the dance floor. Aware that he radiated uneasiness, Peter developed a talent that astonished observers who knew him. Obviously the man has far more going on internally than is suggested by his stilted conversations. There is hidden depth to Peter, but his words seldom reflect the grace and sensitivity he shows when dancing. This is a relationship for a woman who can reap the rewards of nonverbal communication.

A man's movements and gestures are generally the first Love Codes you will have the opportunity to observe. Whether you are making polite party conversation or dancing with a stranger at a disco, notice how he walks, stands, sits and shakes hands, and you will be way ahead of the game in detecting what he'll be like in an intimate relationship. Notice the common threads that allow you to weave together an entire tapestry of his personality. Taken together, these clues let you know whether he is confident, able to make a commitment, and genuinely concerned about your needs − or quite the opposite in all cases.

2

The truth is written all over his face

Beauty may only be skin deep, but the portrait that is etched into a man's face suggests a great deal about the personality beneath the surface. Indeed, it is said that in the early years of our lives we have the face that Nature has given us but that as we age, we develop the face we earn. In the passage from adolescence to adulthood, our behaviour and attitudes are slowly stamped upon our features until they become a map of the past and a blueprint of the future.

Unless he wears a veil over his head the Love Codes in a man's face can be no more readily disguised than his posture or the way he holds his hands. The look in a man's eye, the set of his mouth, his wrinkle lines, and the way he smiles are all enlightening.

Study your man's face carefully and answer the following questions, then read about the characteristics that usually accompany those facial expressions:

- Does he have a wide-eyed or a jaded look?
- Does he look directly at you or avoid your gaze?
- Are there crow's-feet around his eyes?
- When he is not speaking, are his lips sealed tight or are they slightly parted?
- Does his mouth turn up or down?
- Does he have laughter lines around the mouth or frown lines across his forehead?
- Is his smile open and wide or always slightly guarded?
- Does he sometimes obstruct his facial features with his hands as he talks to you?

THE EYES – THE MIRROR OF HIS SOUL

Through the ages, the eyes have been called the mirrors of the soul and indeed they may be a man's most revealing feature. When two people make eye contact, they exchange a message that is more meaningful than words, for the eyes are not only our portals to the outer world, they are the pathway to our inner world as well.

Surreptitiously study your man's eyes for clues to what is buried inside. Do his eyes reveal disdain or curiosity, deep sorrow or steely anger, genuine humanity or a sense of wonder?

RAY: HE'S GOT ROVING EYES

Shirley: *What first drew me to Ray was that rugged square jaw and his thick, sensual lips. There was an intensity to his gaze that was very appealing, but he didn't seem to pay much attention to our conversation. His eyes darted back and forth around the room as he watched partygoers arrive and leave. Occasionally he would look directly at me, but only for a moment. Most of the time he seemed more interested in just about everything else going on around him.*

By constantly glancing away from her, Ray sent a clear message to Shirley that he had no real interest in her. In general, it is wise to steer clear of a man too preoccupied with himself to relax with others.

The Love Codes that Ray emits are particularly negative because obvious insecurity lurks behind his constant scrutiny of others at the party. He is so fearful of missing something that he fails to notice what is right in front of his eyes. Such a man will always be chasing after the pot of gold at the end of the rainbow.

Seeing other Love Codes in his eyes

Direct eye contact

The attentive man who looks you straight in the eye as you talk is genuinely interested in creating an intimate exchange of ideas and emotions. Honest and sincere, he willingly drops his defensive shield when he is attracted to a woman and lets you know that, for the moment at least, you are the only other person in his world.

Unblinking stare

There is a big difference between a man who maintains appropriate and relaxed eye contact and one who is virtually staring at you. An unblinking gaze places you under a powerful microscope and the fact that it makes you uncomfortable is of no real concern to him. If you are interested in a relationship with a powerful and single-minded man, this could be the man for you, but you'll have to realise that he is rather secretive and unyielding in many areas.

Indirect gaze

He's looking at your chin, shoulder, forehead, neck – almost anywhere except your eyes. And although he's definitely interested in getting to know you better, he's hampered by self-consciousness and shyness. A man like this is seeking reassurance and is generally good relationship material when he finds a woman who inspires his confidence.

Shifty eyes

A man who narrows his eyes in doubt and darts his gaze from side to side is nervous and suspicious. Perhaps the events of his life have given him reason to distrust others, but in a relationship you will find it very difficult to get him to accept your unqualified interest – he'll always be wondering what you're really after.

Wink

Initially used as a playful come-on, this is the action of a man who's direct about letting you know that he's really interested. As you get to know him a little better, you'll discover whether he uses the occasional wink to add just the right amount of suggestiveness to a conversation – or whether it is a too-cute gimmick that he uses so often it loses its appeal and signals that he is ill at ease.

EYEBROW RAISING ISSUES

A man's eyebrows are often very expressive, carrying almost as many clues to his personality as the eyes themselves.

- Knitted eyebrows are the trademark of a man overly concerned with responsibility. Shrewd and analytical, he selects the women in his life carefully, often for pragmatic reasons as much as emotional ones. His inability to relax can become irksome but at least this man is not put off by commitment.

- Raised eyebrows suggest a man who is optimistic and filled with wonder about the world. He is appreciative of the virtues of others and enthusiastic about trying new things. If those eyebrows remain raised for a long period of time, it could be a flirtatious gesture to let you know he is quite taken with your beauty and intelligence.

- The man who raises just one eyebrow is a bit of a mischief maker and tends to be sceptical about many things, including relationships. But he is an acute observer, and if his caustic remarks about life's contradictions amuse you, you will find him witty and charming.

THE WAY HE SMILES

Will your man be generous of spirit or stingy with his affection? Is he provocative or sexually tense? Sensual or explosively passionate? A man's smile, the way the muscles in his mouth move and the set of his lips add important information to the words that he speaks.

Laugh and the world laughs with you

How a man expresses mirth is a function of his capacity to experience joy and happiness. A full and spontaneous smile signals a man who is relaxed and content with himself – and is genuinely interested in you, too. Beware the begrudging smile or the smirk, and steer clear of the grim personality too self-absorbed to smile at all.

27

JULIAN: HE MERITS A BRUSH-OFF

Olivia: I was rather underdressed at a gallery opening peopled by a very trendy crowd, but I was determined to have fun anyway. I noticed an interesting-looking man wearing overalls and a beret who was studying the canvasses intently, and walked over to say hello. But he gave me an almost withering once-over with his eyes, smirked slightly, and barely acknowledged my greeting. Later, I noticed that he was still smirking at everyone he spoke to.

The man whose lips are imprinted with a smirk is rather conceited and harbours notions of false superiority. Cynical about the value of others, he tends to be sarcastic and in a relationship he will denigrate your achievements to preserve his own sense of accomplishment. Better to avoid this man from the beginning.

What other smiles reveal

Ear-to-ear grin

Here's a good-humoured man whose wide open smile can light up a room. It's the mark of someone who is not afraid to express every last bit of pleasure, the type who looks optimistically at everything. Such a sense of joy and well-being is contagious and in a relationship you will probably find yourself more upbeat than usual. At times, his flamboyance can be a bit overbearing but he is so well-intentioned that you'll have to forgive him that trait.

Frozen

Like a wax figure, this man looks as though the expression he is wearing is moulded on his face. Although a frozen smile looks real at first, you'll quickly discover that it is actually unchanging, an indication that this man is trying to shield his feelings from others. Chances are that this man is none too happy with himself, and therefore not likely to be happy in a relationship, either.

Mouth closed

Unless he wears dental braces and is a bit uncomfortable about them, a tight-lipped smile is usually the indication of a repressed and withdrawn man. Fearful of losing his emotional balance, he is detached and won't let himself get too deeply involved in the give-and-take of genuine love.

Relaxed and natural

A man who has a warm smile and uses it readily at appropriate moments in a conversation has a real knack for putting others at ease. As you get to know him better, you may find that he smiles at you the moment you walk into the room, a non-verbal way of repeatedly reminding you that he is delighted to see you.

LOOK AT HIS LIPS

A man's lips can be as revealing as his smile. Does he bite his lower lip? That is a classic sign of nervousness, usually suggesting that he is suppressing something he knows he really should say. Other Love Codes can be found in these expressions:

- **Parted Lips:** This is the sign of someone who is open and receptive to you. He is interested not only in what you say but who you are, asks questions that enable him to learn more about you, and listens closely to your answers.

- **Tight-Lipped:** Tight-lipped men usually have a lot on their minds but they seldom reveal any of it. Because they are almost ready to burst with emotion, they frequently develop stress-related symptoms, including headaches and ulcers. Don't count on this man for a relationship built on deep trust or emotional honesty.

- **Upturned Corners:** An eternal optimist, he has a good sense of humour and sees things in a positive light. In a relationship, as in other dimensions of his life, he is genial and good-natured, and his good humour can be infectious and refreshing. By contrast, the man whose lips turn down is disappointed in the world and rather jaded as a result.

- **The Pouter:** The pouter suffers life's indignities in silence but nonetheless feels deeply pained by them. You'll find that he is empathetic and can be a great listener, but he has not dealt effectively with his own problems and must rely on you to provide the strength and reassurance that he lacks.

- **Lick Those Lips:** A flagrantly sexual gesture, this man is letting you know that he finds you delicious company. If he is subtle about his interest, he'll run his tongue over his lips in a few quick gestures as you talk; a cruder version of the same gesture is to run his tongue long and slow from one corner of his mouth to the other. Unless you are interested in sex only, not romance, don't pursue this fellow.

- **Trembling Lips:** A man's lips may often tremble just before he expresses frustration or anger. Because he is uncomfortable with strong emotional expressions, he tries to control them, but instead they build up inside until the point of explosion. Dealing with a man who frequently works himself up to such a charged state is no easy task so be prepared to handle him with kid gloves.

WRINKLES: READING BETWEEN THE LINES

The lines in a man's face are a veritable road map of his emotions, from joy to sorrow. The imprints left by the most frequent expressions of his face cannot be disguised or camouflaged, making them a very useful tool of analysis.

Here are some of the most visible wrinkle marks to look for:

- **Crow's-Feet:** Crow's-feet crinkling from the corners of his eyes divulge a splendid sense of humour and adventurousness and hint at mischievousness as well. If you meet a man in a sombre or professional environment, his initial manner may not reveal the depth of his wit. But those crow's-feet tell you that it is well worth getting him out of the office and into a more relaxed social situation.
- **Furrowed Brow or Frown Lines:** This suggests a man with a lot of personal and professional concerns, perhaps because he tends to involve himself too deeply in other people's problems. Although he cares a great deal about others, he is a worrier who considers his every move before taking any action.
- **Laughter Lines:** Although sometimes you may wish this man took life a little more seriously, someone who appreciates good humour is usually a safe bet for loving. You can't go too far off the mark pursuing a man who looks at the lighter side of misfortune and will help you turn disappointment into opportunity.
- **Cheek Lines:** These are the lines of a man with a lot of life experience. He has seen both the good and the bad side of his fellow humans, and the events of his life have given him a strength of character that is admirable in a crisis. If you're looking for a man who knows who he is and what he wants, this is the gentleman for you.

- **Wrinkle Free:** Either this man has led an extra-ordinarily sheltered and carefree life or he has an overzealous ability to avoid experiencing emotion. Traditional notions of beauty identify the wrinkle-free man as an attractive catch, but the fact is he has few deep feelings to probe. He lives life at a distance, more an observer than a participant, and has little experience with the euphoria or heartbreak of true passion.

FACING UP TO OTHER LOVE CODES

Turning red

A man who reacts to an annoying situation by turning bright red harbours such exasperation and rage that he is a clear threat to those nearby. Unless he has been drinking or lying too long in the sun, a man's face usually turns red when adrenaline pours into his system and the blood pounds in his veins. Never provoke a man in this state because he may become verbally, or even physically, abusive. If you see him turn red over small slights, a relationship is certain to turn into constant combat.

The look of power

Chin pushed forward, jaw almost frozen, corners of the mouth sharply turned down, this is the expression of a man with pugnacious determination. A look coveted by men like Mussolini and Richard Nixon, these men are preoccupied with power. Needless to say, they are rarely willing to compromise. And if they do negotiate with you, it's only a shrewd tactic designed to get what they want.

The blush

Not to be mistaken for the turning red, a blush is a mild pink sheen on a man's cheeks and is often accompanied by a sheepish, hidden smile. The man who often blushes tends to be playful and open to suggestion but is somewhat bashful. The best match for the blusher is a strong woman who can guide him into previously unexplored romantic realms.

White heat

A man whose blood has drained from his face is either terrified or furious. Better gauge the source of his emotional reaction. If it is much more trivial than his response to it, it will be hard to get him to deal rationally with his fears or anger. There is no talking reason to a man in this state; in fact, if this is his frequent reaction, it is seldom worth trying to talk to him at all.

Flaring Nostrils

This is a sign of a man who can be more easily excited and aroused than most. Highly emotional, sometimes to the point of becoming temperamental or moody, he does not try to conceal his feelings and lets you know just what he's thinking and feeling. Occasionally he'll explode in anger, but the feeling doesn't last very long; more often, he is a man of passion and is drawn to strong women and intense relationships.

Facial tics and twitches

The more tics and twitches a man has, the more nervous and repressed he is. Most unconscious facial tics are the result of deep psychological traumas that he has buried rather than confronted. He is likely to be quirky and neurotic in a relationship, and unless you are prepared to cater to his needs and wants, it is wise not to get too deeply involved with him.

Facial Love Codes, then, can offer you a tremendous amount of information about your man. Where he directs his eyes, how he gestures with his eyebrows, the readiness with which he smiles and the set of his lips add to the information you have already garnered from the way he moves.

With these movements and facial Love Codes as our foundation, we'll delve further into his personality by studying the choices he makes and how he behaves in a number of everyday situations. Remember, every new Love Code you observe helps clarify the ones that came before, an important point as you continue the task of assessing a man's strengths and weaknesses.

3

Is he tailor-made for you?

It is said that clothes make the man. Certainly they create a powerful first impression and provide many clues about his personality and his traits as a lover. A man who knows how to dress with flair and a sense of personal style can be extraordinarily attractive to women even if he is not conventionally handsome. And, conversely, a classically good-looking man who is careless about his appearance and indifferent in his choice of clothing can turn women off without understanding why.

Fortunately for all concerned, women are drawn to men who dress very differently – someone who swoons over a man in a grey flannel suit may be totally turned off by the bohemian who wears jeans, a corduroy jacket, and a beret. The aim of this chapter, then, is to alert women to the Love Codes lurking behind particular clothing styles. After that, you must decide whether those clues reveal a personality type that appeals to you.

CLOTHES MAKETH THE MAN

A true understanding of your man begins with the recognition that his clothes reveal more than just his sense of fashion. Pay careful attention and you can also learn how he feels about intimacy. Clothes, after all, are what's physically closest to him and if he is contemptuous or indifferent to them, it could be cause for worry. On the other hand, if he treats them with reverence and respect, you'll want to make an effort to know this man better.

1. **Are his clothes strewn about the floor and the nearest chair or hung neatly in the wardrobe?**

- In a relationship, a man who scatters his clothes haphazardly is likely to be casual and a bit irresponsible, but enthusiastic and easygoing as well.
- A compulsively neat man tends to be stubborn and unyielding in close relationships and it can be very difficult to get him to change.

2. **Are the clothes in his wardrobe ready to be worn or do some of them have broken zips and missing buttons?**

- A man who keeps his clothes in good working order is responsible and willing to make commitments – and stick to them.

37

3. **When an item of clothing tears, does he hold it together with a safety pin, repair it himself, or send it off to the tailor?**

- A man who does his own sewing is independent and capable of taking care of himself. If you need to maintain a degree of independence even in a committed relationship, this man is a good choice.
- The man who uses a tailor knows his limitations and isn't ashamed to consult the experts. And he has enough respect for you not to expect that you will do his sewing for him.

4. **How many times will he wear an item of clothing before sending it out to be cleaned?**

- A compulsively clean man may be too fussy to want to involve himself in a relationship, which inevitably has certain messy components.
- If his clothes are dirty, it is an indication that he doesn't care about himself and is trying to avoid attention from women, too.

5. **Does he arrange the shirts in his wardrobe by colour, sleeve length, or appropriate usage? Or is there no discernible pattern whatsoever?**

- A well-organised wardrobe indicates a man able to assume responsibilities, but you may find him a bit staid in his approach to life and love.
- A man whose clothes are chaotically arranged is often playful and spontaneous in a relationship, but his inability to find the shirt he wants to wear or get to places on time may drive you batty.

6. How many pairs of shoes does he own?

- If you judge him to own an unusually large number of shoes, it may be a sign that he is difficult to satisfy and can never get enough from anyone or anything. Beware of a tendency towards fickleness.
- A man who wears the same shoes over and over again is not lavishly extravagant, either with his money or his affections. He does have a sense of loyalty and consistency, however, which can be very valuable in a relationship.

THE COLOUR OF LOVE CODES

Whether his preferences lean to the sombre or the gaudy, to subtle pastels or electric vibrancy, the colours of a man's clothing provide significant clues about his mood and temperament. Almost everyone has favourite colours, although well-balanced men don't limit themselves to a monochromatic wardrobe; instead they'll opt for a rainbow of colours to suit different moods and different occasions.

Here is what the colour of his clothing reveals:

- **White.** Historically the symbol of virgin purity, a man who wears white may hold rather orthodox views about a relationship. You may find him a bit rigid in his ways, although he will always be honest with you.
- **Black.** This man is sensual and just enough of an outlaw for the right woman to find him very exciting. But a man who dresses mostly in black may be subject to dark moods so be prepared for the moments when he becomes inaccessible.
- **Brown.** The man who wears brown can be sensuous, in an earthy kind of way. Usually, he's got both feet planted on the ground and enjoys the outdoors. Brown suggests a man with solid values and inner strength. You can expect him to be the dependable sort.

- **Red.** The colour of life, this man is flashy, aggressive, and exciting to be with. He constantly seeks new sources of stimulation and is very passionate towards women. He's a good choice if you can respond to him with equal passion.
- **Purple.** A symbol of creativity, this colour reflects a man of extraordinary depth and sensitivity, and you will find that he responds readily to your emotional needs. Sometimes, however, his passion for his art takes precedence over the women in his life and you may find this irritating.
- **Blue.** A man who is fundamentally calm and at peace with himself likes this colour, and you will find his serenity a big plus in a relationship. It is easy to relax and share good times with this man.
- **Green.** The colour of nature and a symbol of renewal, this is a healthy outdoorsman fit for romance and adventure.
- **Yellow.** A spiritual colour, the man who dresses in yellow has good intentions and a respect for humanity. He abides by his promises and you can feel confident that he will keep his commitments to you.

PATTERNS IN HIS LIFE

Once, a man who was concerned with how he dressed was considered vain and even a little vulgar. Today, however, male fashion has assumed a much more significant place in our society. Now we expect our men to know something about clothes and to take some care with their appearance. If they don't we're likely to wonder what's wrong. But if they devote too much energy to it, we're just as likely to be suspicious about their motives.

The result is that today's man is under pressure. That's okay, though – after all, women have endured such pressure for centuries. This section introduces a number of men as it reveals how their approach to clothes tells us what kind of lovers they'll make.

PAUL: A FASTIDIOUS FASHION PLATE

Jennifer: *Paul sent his out-of-season clothes to cold storage and still filled five wardrobes for the summer season alone. He had separate wardrobes for his suits, casual clothes, shirts and overcoats. He also had several drawers with freshly cleaned and neatly folded socks, underwear, and sweaters. Everything he wore was sent to the cleaner or tailor after one wearing.*

Paul took great care in dress, wore expensive cologne, and clearly looked like a man of good taste. Although he often asked my advice about the clothes he wore, he seldom followed it. Even so, he always looked great in whatever he put together – every garment fitted perfectly, from the crease in the trousers to the length of the sleeve. But he never seemed quite convinced; he kept checking his image in mirrors and shop window reflections, making little adjustments here and there.

A man willing to invest time, effort and money in something that he considers important, such as his appearance, will also invest in a woman who is important to him. And the priority he places on being neat and organised about his grooming suggests that he is also conscientious about meeting other obligations. The range of clothing in his wardrobe identifies Paul as a careful planner prepared to respond to any situation appropriately.

Beware, however, of two negative Love Codes here – compulsiveness and narcissism.

- **Compulsiveness.** Paul's fastidious approach to clothes borders on the extreme, and such methodical behaviour often translates into a cold and distant manner with others. Threatened when his strategic plan for living is interrupted, a highly compulsive man

41

cannot enjoy spontaneous activities and prefers his personal relationships to be equally rigid. The drive towards perfection also reveals low self-esteem and self-criticism, suggesting that Paul may be over-compensating for his feelings of inadequacy.

- **Narcissism.** Paul is preoccupied with his appearance to the point of narcissism, and a narcissistic man often views a woman as a reflection of his own image. As long as your appearance flatters his image and you are willing to support his ego, he will gratefully share his comfortable life with you. Once you deviate from his methodical plan, however, he will find a reason to leave the relationship in order to regain control over himself.

MARK: THE MAN WHO REFUSED TO CHANGE

Joanna: *When I first met Mark he made a terrific impression. A successful executive with a go-ahead advertising agency, he was tall, robust, friendly and very good-looking, and he dressed in a well-tailored business suit, shirt and tie.*

In the year that I knew him, however, things began to sour for Mark. The ad agency was bought out by one of its flashier competitors and slowly some of the old staff were replaced. Mark's new boss pointed out that a more stylish, less formal look was 'in' at the firm and suggested several times that he buy some designer suits and more 'trendy' clothing. Mark refused to do it. It wasn't long after the buyout that some of his accounts were given to others.

Change is an inevitable part of life, and a man who cannot cope with it may also have difficulty sustaining a mature relationship. By stubbornly dressing as he pleased, Mark jeopardized his professional goals, a questionable price to pay for maintaining his individuality. Some degree of conformity is invariably necessary in a corporate structure, and by announcing that he is not a team player, Mark sabotaged his own success, perhaps because he did not feel worthy of it. In a relationship he may repeat the pattern, stubbornly insisting on doing things his own way, regardless of how you are affected.

BILLY: JUST A KID AT HEART

Beatrice: *Whether we were going to a film or going out to dinner with my parents, Billy always showed up in faded blue jeans, a T-shirt, running shoes, and usually a baseball cap. He laughed about it and told me proudly that he hasn't owned a suit since his Communion. Although I was charmed by his refusal to be influenced by the fashions of the times, I also got irked because nothing ever seemed special enough to be worth getting dressed up for.*

Day in and day out, this eternal adolescent wears the same outfit – jeans, T-shirt and sneakers. A study in casual dressing, a special occasion for Billy means adding a shirt to the outfit. If you refuse to be influenced by the opinions of others, and are willing to play a maternal role with a man who would rather still be a teenager, then go ahead. Like an adolescent, he can be good company when he chooses to be, but be prepared to cope with his rebellious and moody streak. Any attempt to change him or make demands will be met with typical adolescent hostility.

WILLIAM: TAKING STOCK OF HIMSELF

Louise: *William's single-minded determination was most visible by his willingness to wear the company uniform – during the working week he was never out of the dark, well-pressed suit and tightly knotted Hermes tie that seemed absolutely de rigueur at his firm. Even on holiday his outfit was always carefully co-ordinated. Sometimes he'd wear a pastel shirt but always with dark trousers. His idea of being a little playful was to wear red braces and once in a great while, Bermuda shorts.*

William's conservative mode of dress symbolises his conservative values. He's a team player and that's what he wants from a lover, too. Although he may sow some wild oats in his early twenties, he believes in the virtues of home and family, and within a few years will seek a conservative woman to whom he can commit. Be warned, though, that he has very traditional notions of a woman's role. He'll expect you to conform to rules that govern how you dress, the activities you pursue, where you live, and your social obligations to his clients and colleagues.

DOUGLAS: HE WEARS HIS HEART ON HIS SLEEVE

Maria: *There was just no predicting Douglas. He was a very attractive man and he'd often pick me up for a date clean-shaven, wearing a nicely cut jacket, dark trousers and carefully polished shoes. He'd take me by the arm and we'd stroll together like an elegant couple about town. Sometimes, though, he'd appear at the door with two days' growth of beard on his face, looking as though he had slept in the dishevelled and torn clothing he was wearing. At those times he just seemed mad at the world.*

Douglas is an emotional dresser who looks exactly the way he feels. Such a man is capable of great passion and when he feels good about himself, life together can be wonderful. But be prepared for his moments of rage, too, when you can do nothing right in his eyes. A man of such extremes is deeply needy and, as a result, very loyal to the woman who gives him the love and attention he craves. But do not expect him to change significantly. At bottom he is a self-centred person whose greatest concern is with his own feelings. Your emotions will always come second.

CHARLES: FROM RAGS TO RICHES

Sue: *Charles really aspired to be acknowledged as a wealthy man. Once he confided to me that he had come from a poor family and I guess he'd never looked back. He always wore silk shirts with double-breasted suits handmade in Italy. A casual occasion to him meant a time to dress in co-ordinated casual clothes. He is the only man I ever knew who always wore rings on his fingers and gold chains around his neck. I never saw him take off that jewellery.*

Money is the driving force in this man's life – he considers it his greatest achievement and has no compunctions about flaunting it. A straightforward lover, he'll lay his cards on the table and let you know just what he wants from a relationship and what you'll get in return. Maybe he's looking for good times and sex; maybe he wants to parade you about as his escort; or maybe he wants a supportive and congenial confidante. Although his ability to verbalise his expectations clearly earns this man serious consideration, his cool rationality also signals the fact that he is compartmentalising your relationship. It is often difficult to have a deep emotional involvement with a man like this.

PHIL: IF YOU'VE GOT IT, FLAUNT IT

Rachel: *Phil's mode of dress just oozed sexuality. He wore sleeveless T-shirts in the summer and when he had to wear sports shirts, he kept them open halfway down his chest. He was muscular and well-built, but his tight trousers embarrassed me a bit. I could practically see the outlines of his sexual organs.*

The clothes of the provocateur are designed to reveal as much flesh and muscle as possible. Although he may be exaggerating his sexual confidence somewhat, this man is ready, willing and able to perform. However, such blustery showmanship often hints at an insecurity that results in a preference for sexual fun over commitment. If you want a wonderful one-night stand, he's available, but start talking about future plans and he'll head right out the door.

JONATHAN: LABEL HIM INSECURE

Amanda: *It took me a long time to understand why Jonathan would spend £100 on a shirt that hung on him like a sheet. Or just what he saw in a black overcoat that made him look like a Russian cossack. Finally I realised that what counted to him was the name on the label – as long as an outfit was designed by Armani, Calvin Klein, or another famous designer, he felt comfortable wearing it.*

A man who wears only designer clothes is often someone who places a high priority on status and fashion but doubts his own ability to judge attire that flatters him. Such emotions often extend beyond clothing to many other realms of his life. He may be overly concerned with making the right impression and cater too much to the opinions of others. A man who is preoccupied with pleasing others, however, may be unduly critical of you. Unable to accept himself fully, he is inclined to judge others harshly as well.

ANDY: A SINGULAR SENSATION

Pamela: *Andy's choice of clothing never failed to astonish me. One day he showed up in an electric blue tuxedo. The next time we had plans to go out, he arrived wearing a red leather bow tie, polka dot braces and purple suede shoes. The amazing thing is that these composite outfits work together! He's got a real sense of style, one that is uniquely his own. It really takes a lot of confidence to stretch the boundaries of convention the way Andy does.*

Although his outfits defy description or imitation, an artist's hand obviously lies behind the assemblage worn by the creative dresser. Despite colours that often clash, fabrics that are mismatched and jarring pattern combinations, this man manages to look really enticing. Andy's clothes reveal him to be a person of high energy and hot emotion. He's a bit of a show-off but in intimate surroundings you'll find him very attentive to your needs. Like any artist, the creative dresser tends to be overly sensitive, but if you walk gingerly around points of sensitivity – and never, ever criticise his appearance – you will find him open and responsive.

DRESSED TO A 'T'

Once the word T-shirt was virtually synonymous with undershirt. Now, however, the T-shirt has evolved into a fashion commodity; it is worn to broadcast social, personal and political messages. Subtle Love Codes are buried in those messages.

Laden with slogans

Whether they are humorous ('My Parents Went To Hong Kong But All I Got Was This Lousy Shirt'), political ('Save the Whales') or ethnic ('Kiss Me, I'm Italian'), a T-shirt with a slogan is a boast to the world. Whether he wants to show off his sense of humour, communicate his origins or state his political viewpoint, this man is proud of what he's got to say. He's an equally upfront and confident lover, although more than a little opinionated.

Announcing where he's been

A wayfarer who has collected shirts from exotic destinations is likely to be sentimental in a relationship and determined to keep your interactions from growing stale. He'll expect you to be as responsive to change and novelty as he is.

Plain white or coloured T-shirts

Anonymous and casual, this man reveals little of himself in public and may be difficult to draw out in a private relationship as well. Although his resistance to trendy fads is refreshing, he doesn't have the originality to set many of his own trends, either.

ON THE BEACH

There is no place except the beach where a man is permitted to publicly display so much of his body. The choice he makes between baggy trunks, a tight bikini and a wet suit, may reveal more than he realises.

Trunks

The man who wears a sturdy pair of trunks to the beach is practical and interested in things that are functional, not glamorous. Off the beach, that translates into a man who values hard work and concrete activities. If you're a solid, down-to-earth woman looking for one of the same, there's opportunity here.

Skimpy Briefs

The skimpy brief-wearer is a social gadabout who loves parties, dancing, drinking and wild women. He is socially at ease and loves to be the centre of attention. Women are drawn to his charismatic personality and he genuinely enjoys their companionship. But marriage? This man may not be ready.

Wet suit

The serious athlete comes to the beach to swim, not to lie aimlessly on the sand. Be careful: if his rigorous exercise regime means he has no time for leisure, it may also leave him little time for you. But all that attention to exercise and health has made this man muscular, attractive and strong; if you can perform at his pace, you may find a positive, serious relationship here.

JEWELLERY SHOWS

The man who wears jewellery is confident enough about his own masculinity to enjoy the decorations without feeling that his manhood will be called into question. Rings, chains and, of course, watches are all very popular among men. Here, then, are some of the more common Love Codes disclosed by a man's jewellery.

PHILIP: STEEPED IN HISTORY

Monica: *Philip wore a couple of nice pieces of jewellery and rarely went out without wearing them. Each one had its own history. There was a gold chain given to him by his ex-wife, a thin string bracelet that the daughter of a former girlfriend had made, and an old watch from his deceased father.*

Many people treasure mementos and nostalgic reminders of important relationships and experiences in their life, which signal an ability to be emotionally caring and involved with others. By wearing jewellery with a strong emotional history, Philip was honest about the strong attachments of his past, an indication that he is forthright about his previous involvements and honest in this one. Be sure that this man is not so emotionally caught up in old love affairs that he cannot open himself up enough to accept a new one.

The flasher

A man who wears a lot of rings, bracelets, and necklaces generally wants to announce to the world that he has arrived. Often such a man comes from humble origins and spends lavishly – in a showy sort of way, of course – so that others know the degree of his material success. He will shower the woman he loves with generous presents but expects her to show gratitude publicly by enhancing his own image.

Understated success

A man who wears only one or two inconspicuous pieces of jewellery is someone secure with his position in life. He doesn't feel a need to prove his authority and power and will treat you more like an individual than another lovely acquisition.

THE RING OF TRUTH

Rings have long been used to symbolise personal taste, social position and financial standing. More than any other piece of jewellery, rings have associations with permanence. Wedding rings are the classic example, of course, but rings also symbolise family heritage and club affiliations.

Signet and family crests

This man has a strong sense of his own past and is understandably proud of his ancestry. Perhaps he has genuine reason to be proud, but you'll want to make sure that he is not an under-achiever resting on the laurels of his ancestors.

Wedding rings

Unless you've got a strong masochistic streak or a passion for playing with fire, don't risk the heartbreak of this involvement. Be particularly wary if his wedding band is large and ornate – he's announcing his marital status loud and clear. On the other hand, if he slips the ring nervously on and off his finger, he could be unconsciously questioning his commitment to the marriage. If you're prepared to deal with that ambivalence, then proceed with caution.

Neither rings on his fingers nor bells on his toes

This man is basically a free spirit who doesn't want to feel encumbered by his past. The affiliations of yesteryear are not particularly important to him, an indication that he might also be elusive about making a commitment in the future.

WATCH OUT!

A watch these days is as much status symbol as it is a timepiece and there are many Love Codes lurking behind the watch he chooses to wear.

Pocket watch

Here is a man with a romantic spirit who cherishes mementos of the past. Applause for the gentleman who fancies an old-fashioned approach to living; he has enough respect for time to build a lasting relationship slowly, wooing you along the way with flowers and love poems.

Alarm watch

By contrast, a man wearing a watch with an alarm is a man of fast-paced action. He's decisive and direct, some would say calculated, in large part because his pressing day allows no time for missed deadlines. The woman who becomes involved with him will have to adhere to his tightly structured life and professional agenda. This man does not have much time for spontaneity.

No watch

A man who wears no watch at all is fiercely proud of his individualistic ways. Although he boasts about his autonomy and likes to claim that time has no control over him, he is actually very dependent on others. That's why he always seeks to engage strangers in conversation, approaching them with the same opening line: 'Excuse me, do you have the time?'

This tour of the Love Codes in clothing and jewellery provides important guidelines for predicting a man's behaviour in a relationship. These early clues are particularly important because they are so easy to observe. Both the man who dresses with extreme care, down to the last finishing touch of jewellery, and the one who expresses indifference about clothing, reveal far more about themselves than they realise.

4

The first date

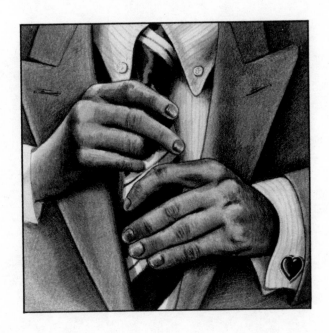

It is perfectly natural for both you and your escort to feel a bit nervous on your first date, so try to make allowances for the discomfort inherent in the situation. Harsh judgments are inappropriate, although it is wise to remain alert to the cues that signal your man's emotional character.

Whether he arrives early or late for a first date, the tenor of your conversation and the way the decisions about your activities get made all tell you a lot about your new romantic possibility.

WHERE TO GO AND WHAT IT MEANS

The first serious decision the two of you will have to make is where to go on your first date. If his approach is traditional, he'll call with a specific invitation and make all the reservations. A man with a strong egalitarian bent might say instead, 'I'd really like to see you. What sort of activities are you interested in?' And then a rather passive individual is likely to act this way:

BARRY: DECISIONS, DECISIONS

Mary: *I don't consider myself the kind of person who takes charge, but with Barry, I had to be. No matter what, whether it was the play we chose or the restaurant we ate at afterwards, Barry kept saying, 'It's up to you'. Finally, when we got back to my place, he actually asked me if he could kiss me. Know what I said? 'It's up to you'. You should have seen him then.*

Men like Barry are products of environments where, as children, they were dominated by their family, particularly their mother. Unable to assert themselves as adults, they seek to recreate this condition of powerlessness in order to substitute the woman they're with for their mother. There's one significant difference, however. This kind of subtle manipulation is also an expression of anger, well hidden beneath the surface. It's the rage he could never show his mother, but which suddenly might be unleashed upon you. In the final analysis, the very passive man can be the most controlling of all.

In three of the most common dates a man might suggest – drinks, dinner or the cinema – a number of tendencies are revealed:

- **Drink Date:** This man is very cautious about making commitments, or being tied down in any way. He makes a careful evaluation before plunging ahead, but once he has made up his mind, he is steadfast in pursuing a goal.

- **Dinner Date:** Here's a man who is relaxed with people and definitely interested in getting to know you. Although he is open to the possibility of romance, he is not counting on it; for now, he's happy just to chat.
- **Cinema Date:** This man is rather insecure about his conversational abilities and needs time to relax before he will open up. Seeing a film together gives him a ready-made topic of conversation after the show. If he suggests coffee or a drink after the film, you know he's warming up!

LOOKING GOOD FROM THE START

Proceed optimistically when:

- He insists that you plan the first evening together.

This is a man worthy of a fair chance – could be that you have found a man who is genuinely considerate, eager to please and curious about your interests. In any case, you can't lose with this evening. Even if your date is a dud, at least you'll have the chance to do something that *you* enjoy. It's possible, however, that he suffers from a lack of imagination or feels uncertain about his critical judgments. Watch for further evidence.

- He says he loves independent women and asks as many questions about your work as you ask about his.

A man with a contemporary outlook on life appreciates independent women who are able to stand alone both emotionally and economically. If you continue to see this man, you may become frustrated by his unwillingness to allow you to lean too heavily on him. As compensation, however, he is not threatened by your capacity to compete with him as an equal.

- When you run into an old friend, he greets her – or him – warmly, then excuses himself for a few moments to give the two of you a chance to chat.

What a pleasure to be with a man who is not threatened when you briefly turn your attention away from him. Such grace and confidence is rare and should be appreciated.

- He laughs off the annoyances of the evening. Whether the film was sold out, the meal was overcooked or he backed into a car on the way to the theatre, he shrugs and asks that you give him another chance to create the perfect evening for you.

Plans *will* go awry in this world and mature is the man who does not quickly search for a scapegoat to explain away mishaps. The wise man knows that if life gives him lemons, he should make lemonade; any man patient enough to make the best of a misfortune deserves a closer look.

SIGNS TO WATCH OUT FOR

Proceed with caution when:

- He arrives an hour and a half late and says he didn't call because that would have delayed him further.

The unspoken sentiment is that he couldn't be bothered going out of his way to look for a phone or he wasn't concerned enough about you to be on time. This man could turn out to be someone who shirks responsibility or is insensitive to your feelings.

- He dominates the conversation, filling in every lull in conversation with anecdotes and information about himself. Although you find this man genuinely fascinating, the fact that he never asks you a single question begins to grate on your nerves.

Men who talk incessantly about themselves and show no real interest in others can be infuriating, and this may be a sign of self-centredness. But don't jump to hasty conclusions about your date. Perhaps he is just respectful of your privacy and willing to wait until you are ready to reveal yourself. Time will tell.

• He says, 'You're perfect – just the kind of woman I've been looking for.'

Such a line is the stuff of myths and dreams, rarely the reality of genuine relationships. If a man tells you this on your first date, he has most likely placed you on a pedestal of the imagination, a height from which you are destined to fall. Be careful.

• He tells you that he's difficult or has problems with his friends and family because they're difficult.

Women tend not to accept a man's evaluation of himself, especially when they are hoping to see something else there. The fact is that most men will tell you what they're really like and it is wise to believe them. And if they find many other people difficult, it is a tip that they are difficult themselves. If you are willing to accept the challenges of relating to a difficult man, however, life is unlikely to grow dull.

• He tells you that women have become too independent and complains that they aren't willing to work on a relationship or make commitments.

It's a popular notion that today's man is unable to make a commitment. The fact is that many men have the same complaints about women. What you may be hearing from this man is that he has not met a woman who is willing to relate on his terms. Find out what those terms are – maybe you won't find them unreasonable.

- He is critical of your appearance ('You really should have worn something more casual; I'm wearing jeans'); your behaviour ('Tell *me* what you want; *I'll* talk to the waiter'); or your intellectual capabilities ('If you understood anything about nuclear war, you wouldn't say that').

Here is an extremely self-conscious man who is dissatisfied with himself and whose actions are powered by the opinions of others. Because he believes that he is being judged by others at all times, he will try hard to mould you into someone he considers 'appropriate'. A hypercritical man can become very controlling and debilitating to a woman's sense of self-worth.

WILL HE DRIVE YOU CRAZY?

Driving patterns reveal a great deal about someone's mood and their attitudes towards everyday social encounters, and you can become aware of a man's driving behaviour as early as your first meeting. How a man relates to other cars on the road is very much the same way in which he relates to other important people in his life, thus providing significant clues about a future relationship.

MOVE OVER, MARIO ANDRETTI

Anna: *When I first met James he struck me as a coolheaded and rational man who thinks through his decisions carefully and only makes a move once he feels certain that it is right. But on our first date I discovered that his considered approach to life vanishes when he gets behind a wheel! Suddenly he was a racing-car driver, almost never leaving the fast lane on the motorway, weaving in and out of traffic, and honking his horn at the slightest delay. When I asked him to slow down he just laughed it off, saying he's never had a serious accident.*

James may appear to be coolheaded, and in many areas of his life he probably is, but he also has an aggressive streak in his personality and resents authority. A fast driver is expressing pent-up hostility, perhaps in response to a childhood of strict discipline. Approach this relationship with extreme caution. James is clearly unwilling to allow others to set limits for him and will go to extremes to assert his independence. A man who is too selfish to compromise, even at the expense of his companion's discomfort, may be too emotionally immature to make a loving commitment.

A look at other driving patterns

The slowcoach

At the other end of the spectrum is the driver who travels way below the established speed of the road. A man who feels timid and unsure behind the wheel has not learned to take control of a situation. He envies others who constantly surpass him but never seizes the opportunity to use what power he has. In a relationship, the slow driver is likely to fear making the first move and will rely on you to take charge.

The law-abider

Here is a mature man who feels no need to prove himself with a macho performance on the road. But he is not fearful of asserting himself, either. He views driving as a practical matter designed to get him where he's going. Generally such a driver is dependable and thorough, a man who does most things in moderation. In a relationship he is likely to be even-tempered and controlled; although not a man for a woman who seeks great passion, his reliability will be a joy to many.

The heavy honker

His hand is positioned on the horn just waiting to blast pedestrians or other drivers for perceived transgressions. This man's frustration level is low and he vents his aggressions without restraint. Away from the wheel, he finds screaming and shouting at others the best technique for getting his own way. Ditch this man. As ineffectual and impotent in a relationship as he is on the road, he's going nowhere but could drive *you* crazy.

The gear changer

Confident and in charge, the man who always drives a manual car doesn't like to take a lot of shortcuts in his life. He relies on his instinct, goes the extra mile to accomplish things in his own way and is very trustworthy. He handles his relationships with competence, but a caution is in order: don't enter into an involvement with a lot of predetermined game plans. This is not a man who readily asks for or accepts advice.

RESTAURANT LOVE CODES

The way a man handles the bill at a restaurant provides you with an early glimpse at his attitudes towards money. If he pays with cash, ask why, in a casual tone of voice. Could be that he's not reporting all his income for tax purposes. Keep alert: A man who is secretive with the government might be secretive with you, too.

On the other hand, it may signal a man with a pay-as-you-go attitude towards life, who hates to incur any debts. Honest and straightforward, he doesn't give in to impulse, and in a relationship you can trust him with responsibility. But you may find his rigid attitude frustrating when you want to buy new furniture or take an exotic holiday.

Some men use credit cards to live beyond their means and then complain about a mountain of debt. A consumer who needs immediate gratification is also a lover without the patience to stick around in rocky times. Unless you are interested in a short-term affair, stay away – this relationship will be filled with constant squabbling. A man who uses a credit card appropriately and conservatively, however, keeps his business affairs in order and usually makes a good catch.

Here are other Love Codes in the way a man pays the bill.

The Traditionalist

It is still customary for a man to pay the bill on the first date, and many men do this simply to avoid awkwardness. But if you feel more comfortable offering to pay – and he seems embarrassed by the suggestion – he is seeking a fairly traditional relationship in which he can play a dominant role.

The Haphazard Approach

The man who produces a wad of notes or whips out his credit card without so much as a glance at the bill may be deliberately trying to impress you. He seems to be suggesting that money is of so little importance that he need not concern himself with something so trivial as the bottom line. If you admire a piece of jewellery in a shop window, he might just go in and buy it for you. This man can be wonderful – providing he has the money to back up his impulses!

On the other hand, he may simply have a casual attitude towards money. He either trusts other people or just doesn't worry about the insignificant errors he is likely to find. He'll be equally accepting and noncritical of you – the kind of man who will think you're beautiful even if you get a bad haircut or gain a few pounds. He won't press you about where you've been or who you've been with.

The Careful Calculator

When the bill arrives, this man studies the prices he has been charged and carefully retotals the whole thing. Inherently distrustful, he believes that if he doesn't keep a close watch, people are certain to make mistakes – mistakes that seldom go in his favour. Steer clear if he believes that people are out to cheat him; his suspicions are likely to extend to you. He'll make you account for any money you spend, whether it is his or yours, and insist on knowing your daily whereabouts.

The Overview

The man who casts his eye over the bill but does not scrutinise it is careful without being overly cautious, self-confident but not flamboyant. He earns high marks for being stable and direct about his objectives while maintaining a healthy detachment towards the world around him. He'll notice your new dress but probably will not go out and buy one for you.

Even Steven

When the bill arrives, this man proposes that you each pay your share. The Love Codes here depend partly on how he handles the situation. If he simply lays down his cash and then waits expectantly for you to do the same, he may view you as one of the boys, a chum rather than an object of romantic affection. On the other hand, if he lets you know that he abides by the principles of equality in other realms of his life as well, then this is your opportunity to be an independent woman.

TIPS ON TIPPING

The way a man tips those who serve him reveals a great deal about his generosity and willingness to share what he possesses emotionally, as well as financially, with others.

The cheapskate

The man who leaves little or no tip in a restaurant, regardless of how good the food and service were, carries a chip on his shoulder that doesn't bode well for a healthy relationship. His refusal to leave a gratuity indicates that he is stingy with his praise and his affections.

This man is cheap but he's no bargain. A man who cheats others feels cheated himself and is too emotionally impoverished to love and nurture a woman. Better stay away.

An appropriate 15 per cent

Whether the service was bad or good, he tips the conventionally prescribed percentage of the bill. Such a man is even-tempered and contented, likes to meet conventional expectations, and refuses to be driven to extremes. In a relationship you can expect him to be fair, consistent, and reliable, but don't look for adventure or excitement. No real highs, but no real lows here either.

Wildly extravagant

Showing appreciation for services rendered is one thing, but this man really goes overboard. Tips consistently over 30 per cent suggest a man who is as insecure as he is well-to-do and feels that no one will appreciate him unless he flaunts his money. Such a man often showers the women in his life with expensive presents. His insecure streak can be a problem in a relationship, though, if he demands constant reassurance and 100 per cent of your attention.

Tipping for insurance

The maitre d' and his favourite waiter are the beneficiaries of this man's generosity, and in the course of the evening you may see him slip notes to the barman, the piano player and the doorman as well. Prudent and sophisticated, this man knows that money makes the world go round; he hands out tips with cool subtlety, and gets top service and a warm welcome wherever he goes. In a relationship, he'll dominate by indulging your every material whim to keep you happy. A woman who values this will feel lucky.

Appreciative tipping

All signals are go for the man who rewards those who go out of their way to please him – especially if he's generous in his appreciation. He's the kind of man who makes a woman feel special by noticing the little things she does for him.

THE FIRST KISS

Kissing is usually the first intimate sexual contact between two people and a perfectly appropriate way of ending a first date. There are Love Codes lodged not only in the way that he kisses but also where and when.

- **Eyes Closed:** Many a man will close his eyes, indicating that he is aroused by amorous fantasy when he kisses you. This man tends to be a romantic and jumps quickly into relationships.
- **Eyes Open:** Some men kiss with their eyes open because they are guarded, cautious and reticent about expressing emotions. He may be the kind of man who seeks to control the relationship.

- **Hard Kisser:** Although his kiss can be exceptionally provocative and exciting, the man with no other kiss in his repertoire is trying to hide his vulnerability by dominating your affair.

- **Tongue Kissing:** Tongue kissing usually accompanies intense arousal and it is a useful gauge of his commitment to an equal relationship. Ideally, he will permit a complete give and take as you explore each other's mouths with your tongues. Be wary of the man so eager to dominate that he literally shoves his tongue down your throat.

- **Public Kisser:** A man who kisses you repeatedly in public feels the need to advertise his sexuality to others, usually because he is plagued by private doubts about how sexy or attractive he appears to be.

- **Caresser:** This is a man who has learned that true sexual power is a function of understatement and subtlety. He's patient and sensitive to your needs, exploring each and every inch as he seeks the spots you find most exciting. His self-assurance indicates his sexual maturity and is often accompanied by the kind of emotional maturity necessary for a viable romantic relationship.

- **The Everybody Kisser:** This man dispenses warm and friendly, but decidedly nonsexual, pecks on the cheek to everyone he meets. He is genuinely open to intimate human contact and eager for love. However, further observation will determine if he's someone who loves 'everybody' but can't commit to the intimacy of 'just one'.

A first date can be the source of an astonishing volume of information. Watch his spending patterns, notice whether he keeps you waiting or is the first to arrive, pay attention to how he drives and who plans your activities together, and always be aware of the dynamics of your conversation.

Many of the Love Codes you observe here will continue to be surprisingly relevant as your relationship evolves. Naturally you will also be reassessing the information as you learn more, but you may also discover that later observations only confirm your first ones.

5

What secrets does his house hold?

A man's home is his castle, the realm in which he reigns supreme. Here he expresses his personal style, makes a statement about how he treats his guests and reveals his quirks, flaws and attributes, often without being aware of doing so. When he invites you to his place, whether it is for drinks, dinner or a torrid affair, he hands you a key that can unlock the secrets of his personality.

To see someone's home is to share his most personal space. There are Love Codes in his living room, his kitchen, his bedroom and his bathroom. Seize the opportunity to snoop, observe, dissect and analyse his furnishings, the paintings on the wall, the pets underfoot, and so forth.

FURNISHING THE CLUES

A man's furnishings and how they are put together offer a map to his style of living. Whether every room is carefully co-ordinated or his entire home is a chaotic pot pourri, there is a message here about what he can furnish if you become involved. After you have noted the overall mood of his place, you'll want to look more closely at each room in order to get more detailed information about this man. And the personal touches he adds to his home after he selects its basic furnishings also help reveal his true colours.

HENRY: A WEEKEND AT THE PALACE

Caroline: *Henry has a beautiful country house estate. The main house faces onto a lake, and large copper and wood sculptures dot the grounds. Inside, it is tastefully furnished, with silk-covered couches and antique tables. Original works of*

71

*art are lit as if they are being displayed in a museum. But there
are no family photos displayed, no newspapers or magazines left
lying around, no personal clothing, not even a used ashtray.
Still, the place is a fantasy come true.*

A man with money is a person with almost unlimited
decorating options, and Henry had made a number of
revealing choices in his weekend getaway home. Although
he had selected an elegant decor, he had left no personal
imprint whatsoever on the mansion. Despite the beauty of
the surroundings and the aesthetic appeal of the furniture,
the house felt cold, almost barren. Everything was so neatly
and purposefully arranged that the place did not feel like a
home at all.

Caroline: *Although our time together was very romantic,
Henry was quite tied up with work, and we met mostly over
meals prepared by his housekeeper. He drove me home Sunday
evening, apologised for having been so distracted and promised
to call soon. When I didn't hear from him after a week, I
phoned and he apologised for being out of touch, saying that he
had been very busy. He told me again how much he had enjoyed
the weekend but hung up without suggesting that we get together
again.*

*It was two full months before he called again and then very
matter-of-factly suggested I come out to the country house for
another weekend. I was flabbergasted at his gall – he just
assumed I would be ready to come back at the drop of a hat!*

Henry's attitude toward Caroline was almost as impersonal
as his home. She was, in fact, only a backdrop to his busy
life, an attractive ornament to further decorate his palatial
home. Although Henry is not malicious, he acts like a
spoiled child. Accustomed to having people around to
service his needs and whims, he views women as useful
implements but brings little tenderness to his interactions.

He is not relationship material for the woman who seeks emotional involvement.

CHRIS: SALVATION ARMY MODERN

Sheila: *Chris was proud that he had never purchased his own furniture. The couch came from his mother's house and his aunt had given him the bedroom suite. A previous tenant had left the lamps and end tables behind, his neighbour donated the kitchen table, and he found the armchair on the street. Books were piled on the floor and records were stored in orange crates.*
The Salvation Army mode of decorating his home reminded me of my very first college flat – but that was 15 years earlier! Chris is a lawyer earning good money and he still lives as though possessions and style just don't matter.

Men who live as though they were still in college may be waiting for just the right woman to help them settle down. If you don't object to a casual style of living and are willing to devote all the energy that personalising his home requires, plunge ahead with this relationship.

Beware, though – this man may have more serious problems such as an emotionally or financially deprived childhood, that continues to shape his adult life. If the latter explains his approach to decorating, he is likely to make you uncomfortable about your own possessions. Such men can not sustain love relationships because they believe they are indulging themselves too much.

PEELING AWAY THE PAINT

1. Is his home comfortable to visit?

Furniture intended for comfort rather than style creates an apartment with a casual atmosphere that makes you warm and relaxed. This is a man who likes to welcome

73

people into his life. He won't try to keep you at arm's length. Expect to spend a lot of time at home with this man.

2. Are his furnishings selected from the pages of a designer catalogue or do they reflect a personal vision?

A home furnished from a catalogue may look magnificent, but you may not feel very comfortable there. In fact, if your man has chosen a designer decor simply to seek the approval of others, he may feel uncomfortable and as ill at ease in a relationship as he is at home. To be fair, of course, some men find designer furnishings very suitable and live harmoniously among them. You will have to determine the motives for his decor before assessing his Love Codes.

A man who designs his own home is an independent thinker who knows what he wants. A woman who can allow him to make most of the decisions will find him a mature, supportive companion.

3. Is there a Grand Plan in his decor or is it a piecemeal assemblage?

Someone whose living environment reflects detailed planning is a man with long-term goals in other areas of his life. He knows what he wants from a relationship and is willing to allow it to evolve in stages.

By contrast, a man with piles of unrelated furniture tends to trust more in serendipity than in ambitious planning. It's tough to get him to make up his mind – and when he does, he might just change it back again – but he is flexible and willing to allow a strong woman to bring order to his life.

4. **Is the seating arranged so that you can face each other comfortably? Must you choose between sitting very close together or on opposite sides of the room?**

If the seating is comfortably and flexibly arranged, this man understands the importance of being adaptable about space. Sometimes you two can come closely together and at other times he is willing to let you go your own way. Being forced to sit close together indicates his tendency to bind you to him in a controlling manner. And if the only places to sit are on opposite sides of the room, this man prefers to keep his distance and is probably not ready for a serious involvement.

5. **Can the lighting be changed to reflect the mood of the evening?**

Dimmer switches or soft lighting suggest a sensual and romantic man who knows how to get you in the mood for lovemaking and probably feels confident in his sexual abilities. Conversely, the man with only harsh, bright lights is rather indifferent to the subleties of romance. He may unconsciously wish to keep his affairs platonic or rather deliberately discourage intimacy.

6. **Does his television set dominate the living room, or is it placed to the side?**

A man whose television set dominates the living room probably uses it frequently and may allow it to substitute for conversation. A television stored somewhat out of sight is likely to be used less often and is not his preferred form of entertainment. If you enjoy curling up and spending a cosy night at home with him, you might enjoy a television addict. Some women, however, find it frustrating and feel neglected by a man who sits constantly before the television.

7. **Is his house neat as a pin, a veritable pigsty, or some-where in-between**

Compulsive neatness carries a hint of hostility with it and suggests a person who doesn't want to be touched or ruffled in any way. He'd rather make you feel a bit ill at ease than encourage you to let your hair down in his presence. The slob is also angry, usually about the mess that he has made of his life. He'll expect you to pick up after him, and his personal history is usually dotted with chaotic involvements.

Somewhere between these extremes is a well-balanced man who knows how to compromise in a relationship. He'll let things slide for a while, but never too long, and the pendulum of his life always swings back towards the centre.

8. **Is there background music playing?**

Combine this with mood lighting and you have a man who is in control of his environment and attentive to every detail. He'll usually want to make all the social arrangements for you both, and he is so reliable that you can be confident that everything has been taken care of. Be prepared to have him call most of the shots.

9. **Do his furnishings reflect the styles of a particular time period? Art deco, Scandinavian modern, Victorian or antique?**

Any home that is strongly influenced by one particular period suggests an occupant who subscribes to many of the beliefs of that time. A man with art deco furnishings, for example, probably has a fondness for the style and culture of the twenties and thirties. Victorian decor reflects a conservative gentleman with Old World values and definite ideas about a woman's proper place.

10. Are his furnishings sparse or crowded together?

A man who furnishes his house sparsely – but not starkly – will give you room to breathe, and he values open space as well. In his relationships, as in his possessions, he knows that one object of substance is worth many that have no real value. This is a man who looks for one person to treasure.

The man whose apartment is crammed with furniture often has a difficult time making judgements and decisions. Because he cannot decide what is really important to him, he prefers to keep everything close at hand. In a relationship, you could find yourself crammed by his ambivalence.

A PICTURE IS WORTH A THOUSAND WORDS

High marks for the man who displays photos of family and friends on his living-room walls, publicly announcing their importance to him. Here is someone who enjoys people and places great value on personal connections and takes pleasure in remembering the positive experiences of days gone by. He's emotionally supportive and good at making a commitment to a woman he loves.

A man who displays tranquil photos of sunsets, mountain-tops and palm-studded beaches appreciates the power of natural beauty and tries to bring a sense of harmony into his home. A rugged outdoorsman or a global adventurer, in mind or deed, he hears nature's call amid the distractions of his urban environment. He may drive you crazy because he'll refuse to argue with you, but you will grow to respect his calm and serene nature.

PLANTS: DISCOVERING HIS ROOTS

A man who cares for plants tends to be nurturing and attentive to detail. Just as he can sense vibrations that tell him his plants need watering, so too can he pick up nonverbal clues sent by the women in his life. Affirmative for the fellow who will tend you patiently when your spirits drop.

Cacti

The man who cultivates cacti has a stark and simple aesthetic sense and most likely a dry sense of humour. He prefers to keep the world at arm's length, though, and

neither asks for nor extends much emotional sustenance. Independence is his virtue, as well as his ability to survive in hostile environments. Also know that, in a relationship, his defences can be very sharp.

Flowering plants

Ever the optimist, the flower-grower believes in possibility where others have only doubt. He enjoys process as much as product, willingly invests in long-shot opportunities, and knows how to cope with disappointment. This man is a good bet for a nurturing relationship.

Artificial plants

Artificial plants are the lazy man's approach to the green finger. He appreciates the aesthetics of plants but doesn't want the burden of daily care. Even more of a responsibility-shirker is the man who has no plants at all. Neither one is a homebody and they much prefer immediate gratification to long-term investments. Unfortunately they will treat you the same way – without much tender loving care.

WHAT KIND OF MAN LIVES HERE?

A man's living room is usually decorated for entertaining and it is the place where he first brings a guest. Because the impression made here is a lasting one, he will try to put his best foot forward. Carefully scrutinising the image portrayed may reveal far more than your man realises.

ALAN: A REPEAT PERFORMANCE

Jennifer: *I was enticed the first time I saw Alan's living room. The grey and salmon decor echoed in the plush wall-to-wall carpeting, the velvet couches and the lithographs of flowers that dotted the walls. The lighting was low, the music soft. The mood was one of subdued sensuality. I felt relaxed and comfortable. I was excited about seeing Alan a second time and, when I returned to his house a week later, it was every bit as beautiful and seductive as I had remembered. It struck me as odd, though, that everything was exactly where it had been a week before. Same lighting, same mood music, even the same floral display. It took me a while to recover from my initial disappointment, but eventually I realised that Alan was rather insecure and reluctant to make radical changes.*

Whether Alan hired a professional decorator or designed the living room himself, it conveys a clear message, 'Here is a man of aesthetic sensitivity and strong sensuality'. He uses warm colours and almost erotically tactile textures. There are no contradictions in his environment – the decor, from the furnishings to the carpeting and the art on the wall, work together to put a visitor at ease.

And yet Alan's carefully cultivated image shielded a fear that desirable women would not be drawn to him. Decor that remains virtually unchanged for long periods of time suggests a man who is afraid of change and not nearly as smooth as he first appears. For a woman confident, spontaneous and patient enough to draw him out, however, there is likely to be a man of some depth here.

GARRY: IS LOVE A GAME?

Debbie: *Garry's living room is loaded with toys and games. He has a trampoline and a tandem exercise bicycle, stacks of board games, water pistols, a dart board and recently he bought one of those old-fashioned pinball machines as well!*

Before we make love, he insists on playing a round of strip poker, and afterwards he likes to relax in the jacuzzi – with a floating backgammon game between us. Even though he is an energetic and passionate lover, I get tired of spending so much time in the playhouse that is his home. And he never stops playing long enough for us to have a serious conversation about our emotional lives. Just once I wish he would talk about our relationship.

Playing games can be a relaxed and amusing way to begin a relationship. By keeping the mood light, Garry guards against rejection and gives you both space to develop bonds without a lot of heavy emotional baggage. As a man like this grows more comfortable and secure, he may be able to communicate more openly.

Beware, however, if the pattern does not change. The compulsive games player is often a man whose emotional development was arrested in childhood. He has difficulty in expressing his feelings and chooses instead to ignore them, concentrating solely on fun and frolic. He won't readily admit his faults and may back out of a relationship at the first sign of rough weather. Many women eventually grow weary of his childishness and move on to more mature relationships.

Other living-room Love Codes

Modern or Hi-Tech

A man who wants to be up-to-the-minute on the latest trends decorates and redecorates his living room as rapidly as styles change. In a relationship, he can be thrilling and fast-paced, a man who likes to get the most out of life. However, don't look for much softness or gentle romance from him. He's a little hard around the edges and will expect you to live with the same concern for style as he does.

Traditional

This is the choice for the man with traditional values who is inclined towards marriage and family. Like his time-honoured and stable possessions, he knows his own mind, is willing to sustain a commitment and remains faithful to those he loves. Perhaps he seems a bit old-fashioned and dull, but many women find his dependability refreshing.

Pot pourri

There is no way to describe the decor of the eclectic designer who lives amid controlled confusion. An independent sort who refuses to be pigeonholed into one category, he has an astonishingly diverse collection of interests and tastes. In fact, the only consistent thing about him is that he is inconsistent! In a relationship, he can be witty and charming but you may wish that he'd take you a little more seriously.

THE KITCHEN: WHAT'S COOKING?

Although the smells of freshly baked bread and apple pie are rarities in most of our kitchens, this room remains the most relaxed and down-to-earth place in the home. Perhaps because of the memories that linger in the scent of a home-cooked meal, the kitchen often conjures up memories of more carefree times. Many people do most of their casual entertaining in the kitchen. The man who invites you into his kitchen is usually prepared to treat you as family, not as a guest.

NEIL: THE COMPULSIVE GOURMET

Patti: *I love gourmet food so I was excited to learn that Neil shared my passion. His kitchen contained all the latest in gadgets and cookware. Unfortunately, he doesn't view cooking as a co-operative venture. I'll offer to help but he always declines sharply, so now I just sit with a champagne cocktail and watch him at work.*

Cooking, for Neil, is an important means of self-expression. A highly skilled chef, he is compulsive about using the finest ingredients and the highest-quality cookware, but insists on total control over a meal. For Neil, cooking is not a means of relaxing so much as a way of performing for others.

Unfortunately, his controlling instincts probably extend beyond the kitchen. Because he feels sure that he has all the answers, Neil does not take kindly to the suggestions of an outsider and needs to have things done his way. This could translate into a suffocating relationship. He'll expect you to exhibit behaviour he deems appropriate and follow the rules he sets down.

Other kitchen Love Codes

Country kitchen

You'll recognise this one by its homely quality: cookbooks on country cooking, recipe boxes and old-fashioned utensils, such as a hand mixer and traditional white crockery bowls. The man who possesses this type of kitchen is easy-going, confident and totally unpretentious. He genuinely enjoys the companionship of women, both in and out of the kitchen.

The drinker's kitchen

If his refrigerator is stocked with beer, wine and mixers (and maybe a bottle of vodka in the freezer), this man either has a drinking problem or just likes to be prepared when friends drop by for the evening.

Look at his shelves and check out the brands of alcohol he

drinks. Imported beers could identify an urbane sophisticate, whereas domestic beer signals someone whose values are middle of the road. What about his wines? The man who knows esoteric wines has a practical and down-to-earth side lacking in the man who stocks nothing but French labels.

Chock-full

There are fresh vegetables in the salad tray, cold meats, carefully wrapped leftovers, and a selection of cheeses and appetisers for nibbling. The meat for the evening's meal is marinating and a shopping list is pinned neatly to the refrigerator door. The well-stocked kitchen reveals a man with a family lifestyle who spends most of his time at home. Stable and well-organised, his relationships are deep and long-lasting, and he takes pleasure in welcoming others to his home – a positive sign for the woman who wants to settle down to a full home life.

Junk-food addict

Inside his refrigerator is leftover pizza, packets of sausages and hamburgers, chocolate milk and soft drinks. Despite all the evidence connecting good health to a sound diet, this man is determined to eat just as he pleases. Although he has a hedonistic and rebellious streak, he knows how to relax and his carefree personality can be a relief from stuffy elitism. He is stubborn but will make few demands on you, as long as you don't try to change him.

The non-cook's kitchen

A man whose refrigerator and cupboard are empty spends little time at home. Active and outgoing, he may enjoy the social whirl of a city or work late so often that he has no time to shop. If he frequently suggests that *you* do the cooking or pick up food to bring to his house, make sure he is willing to reciprocate and doesn't expect you to provide all the sustenance.

THE BEDROOM: PILLOW TALK

Every bedroom has a personality all of its own. It is there that the deepest pleasures and greatest problems of any relationship play themselves out. Whether you are making love with abandon, or nestling together before drifting off to sleep, the bedroom is a place of intimacy and passion. Some men organise their bedrooms for the strictly functional purpose of sleeping, a sign that they are straightforward and direct, albeit minimally interested in sexual pursuits. Others express ambivalent attitudes or unabashed enthusiasm towards sexuality in their decor.

How does your man set the stage for the main event? Begin your search for answers by asking the following questions about his bedroom.

1. What is there to sit on in his bedroom?

a. A chair.
b. A sofa.
c. Only the bed.

2. As an item of furniture, the bed is . . .

a. Only a small part of the room.
b. About equal in proportion to everything else.
c. Completely dominant.

3. What forms of entertainment are available in his room?

a. None.
b. Only a radio.
c. A radio plus a stereo, television or video.

4. What is the temperature of the bedroom?

a. Always too cool.
b. Just about right.
c. Usually too warm.

5. If you want to prop yourself up to read a book or watch television, are there . . .

a. Lots of extra pillows.
b. Just the pillows on the bed.
c. One or two extra pillows.

6. What colour are the walls painted?

a. Soothing, light colours, such as pale blue or yellow.
b. Simple white.
c. Dark shades, such as brown, red or green.

7. What covers the windows?

    a. Curtains.
    b. Shades or blinds.
    c. Nothing.

8. What are his sheets like?

    a. Cotton or cotton blend.
    b. Silk or satin.
    c. Plain white.

9. What sort of tables are there by the side of the bed?

    a. None.
    b. One table on each side.
    c. A table on one side only.

10. What does he use to provide intimate lighting?

    a. Candles.
    b. Lights that dim.
    c. Nothing.

The score

Add the points below for each of your answers, then read the Love Code analysis that follows.

1. a - 4	3. a - 2
b - 6	b - 4
c - 2	c - 6
2. a - 2	4. a - 2
b - 4	b - 6
c - 6	c - 4

5. a - 6	8. a - 4
b - 2	b - 6
c - 4	c - 2
6. a - 6	9. a - 2
b - 2	b - 6
c - 4	c - 4
7. a - 6	10. a - 6
b - 4	b - 4
c - 2	c - 2

[51-60 points]
This man is a very sensual and seductive lover who has created an environment conducive to intimacy and sexual excitement. He will expect you to respond to his efforts with romance and passion and will be very disappointed if you don't. A positive response is appropriate for someone who goes out of his way to please you.

[41-50 points]
A sensitive and considerate lover, this man is not 100 per cent successful in creating a fully sensual experience, but he is clearly trying hard to please you. He will listen to your suggestions and welcome any contribution you can make to improve the love nest.

[31-40 points]
This man has a somewhat ambivalent attitude towards love-making. He doesn't put much extra effort into his bedroom because he doesn't expect his sexual experiences to be extraordinary. And unfortunately, reality usually matches his expectations. He is unlikely to extend himself very far in a relationship.

[20-30 points]
Not much possibility for sexual excitement from this man. Neither resourceful nor particularly interested in the

possibilities of passion, he views the event as a bare and functional experience. No use in drawing sex out, he believes, and that's why he prefers to get it over with fast, without much concern for your satisfaction.

ALEX: EROTIC OR NEUROTIC?

Anna: *When I walked into Alex's bedroom I wondered whether it was an erotic fantasy or a bad joke. There was a white bearskin rug on the bed, mirrors on the ceiling, and giant silver goblets and bowls of grapes by the bed. I was very disappointed to discover that we just didn't click in bed. I had thought he would be as seductive and romantic in bed as he had been with all his clothes on. Instead, he acted as though I wasn't even there.*

Alex had all the right props for a sexual scene in place, but he was unable to provide an experience to match the decor. He hoped somehow to create eroticism with a decorator's formula, rather than breathe life into his set with spontaneous and genuinely affectionate lovemaking. Not all men with sexy bedrooms are insecure, of course. The clue that Alex is more a tease than a performer is simply his excess. That level of boudoir braggadocio almost always masks serious sexual insecurity.

PAUL: THE MAN WHO LIVED IN HIS BEDROOM

Beth: *I found it wonderfully relaxing to spend all of our time together in Paul's bedroom. He had installed a telephone, a television, a stereo and a video there, and when friends dropped by, he usually entertained in the bedroom. In one corner he had set up a small work space where he kept his desk, his files and a typewriter. He had plenty of other space in the house, but he just preferred the cosiness of living in a single room.*

By surrounding himself with his favourite possessions, Paul feels secure and safe. This suggests a contented man who has the ability to make himself comfortable and create an intimate, nurturing space. A good possibility for a woman willing to share it with him. At its extreme, however, this trait can develop into agoraphobia, a fear of the outdoors so severe that the sufferer seldom leaves the sanctuary of the home.

THE BATHROOM: BEHIND CLOSED DOORS

The bathroom is by far the most private room in the house. It is the place where we perform our most basic physical functions, from expelling bodily wastes to bathing and beautifying ourselves. The way a man decorates his bathroom, the cosmetics and toiletries he uses and how much time he spends there all offer clues to his private emotional, social and intellectual life.

BEN: A DESIGNER'S SHOWROOM

Marie: *Ben's bathroom was right off a* Dallas *film set. The thick red towels hung in perfect alignment. The floor was covered with a plush red carpeting with matching red and white velvet shower curtains. Even the toilet seat was carpeted in red! The basin and tub were genuine marble and the bathroom actually had a jacuzzi! The gold-plated rococo fixtures and silk wallpaper completed the opulent picture.*

Only a meticulously organised man, attentive to details, could assemble such a luxuriously appointed bathroom. He announces loud and clear that money is no object where quality is concerned. Ben expects the women in his life to share his taste and values and he sets lofty standards for those he dates. He will see that you have the best that money can buy, but his priorities place appearance over comfort indicating that he is not likely to be as sensitive about providing emotional support to you.

HENRY: THE COSIEST ROOM IN THE HOUSE

Joanne: *Henry's bathroom was the most comfortable and relaxed room in the house. No other room was so well-equipped or elaborately furnished. A telephone had been installed and his clipboard hung on the wall near the bath so that he could work there. There was a small bookcase and magazine rack and recently he even installed a television. We used to laugh and say that his toilet training must have been the happiest time of his life.*

This man loves to surround himself with creature comforts and tends to be rather self-indulgent. His obsession with his own bathroom is excessive enough to suggest an anal-compulsive personality. From the psychological point of view, he tends to be rather rigid about the way he organises his life and resistant to change, even when he knows it is in his own best interests.

Henry's sense of humour about his own anal tendencies, however, is a good sign that he has perspective about himself. Even though it will be difficult to convince him to compromise in a relationship, you may be able to tease him into greater self-awareness.

STEVE: THE SPARTAN

Felicity: *Steve kept absolutely nothing in his bathroom. The towels were plain white and very thin. Sure, there was a toothbrush, soap, a razor and toilet paper in there, but that certainly didn't create the temptation to linger. I don't think there was even a newspaper or a magazine to read on the loo!*

The bare-bones bathroom suggests a man who is much more interested in function than form. He indulges himself in few pleasures of the flesh and thinks life should mean more than lolling around taking bubble baths. You'll find him hard-driving and ambitious and, in a relationship, he'll be steady and loyal but don't count on him to pamper you.

The medicine cabinet

A man's medicine cabinet is loaded with clues about his approach to good health and grooming. Notice whether it is stocked with items for good grooming, natural healing remedies, or pills of every size and shape.

The groomer

A medicine cupboard packed with personal grooming items – razors, shaving cream, after-shave lotion, mouthwash, deodorant and cologne – suggests a man who always keeps up appearances regardless of the circumstances. No matter how poorly he may be feeling, he'll drag himself into the bathroom for a touch-up. It may be hard to see what's going on behind this man's facade but he's tenacious and sturdy, someone who won't be felled by a touch of misfortune. He will be the first to make up after an argument and does his best to pull you out of the doldrums.

The pill popper

Are there lots of prescription drugs inside? Maybe there is something you need to know about his health. If he has a hefty supply of sleeping pills, chances are he is not nearly as cool as he first appears. A man who needs a steady dose of tranquillisers to help him handle life's ups and downs will also burden you with his stress and inability to release his pent-up energies.

Mr Upset

The man who stocks a supply of antacids and indigestion medications suppresses his emotions until they boil inside, and even then he'll take some pills rather than confess what ails him. In a relationship, however, men who experience emotions intensely are often loving and passionate. When their moods are black, they are exhausting to deal with, but in the good times they can be wonderfully clever and witty.

Crisis intervention

If he stocks bandages, gauze, cotton wool, alcohol and iodine, an always-prepared Boy Scout may linger inside your man. A dependable sort who always copes in an emergency, he knows how to bind a wound, tie a tourniquet and stave off infection. Whether the crisis is physical or emotional, here is a man who knows how to administer first aid.

Mind over matter

Behind a practically empty medicine cupboard is an eternal optimist guided by his ability to think positively. 'Get sick? Me? Never!' he boasts, and if there is a touch of arrogance and denial there, the technique seems to work well for him. He doesn't get ill often, won't slow down when he does and believes in being self-reliant and in control.

WHEN HE DOESN'T INVITE YOU HOME

What if he has never invited you to his home? After several months of dating, this is somewhat peculiar and it might be time to find out why. There are any number of explanations, some of them perfectly valid but all of them very revealing. Whatever the reason, it pays to find out what's going on before you become too deeply involved. Here are three of the most likely explanations:

1. He's keeping something hidden

- Perhaps his home is a pigsty, he still lives with his parents or with flatmates, or he is ashamed that he cannot afford anything better. This man is lacking in feelings of self-worth and disappointed in his achievements thus far. Depending on his age, he may still become a great success or you may end up having to help support him.
- He doesn't want you to be dazzled by his riches. Affluent men need to know that a woman loves *him*, not his money. This is usually a sign that he lacks confidence and is not at ease with wealth. It may be difficult for a woman to change his attitude and convince him that he is worth more than his money.
- He doesn't want you to see signs that another woman has recently spent time in his apartment. Maybe he has

an innocent explanation for keeping another woman's clothes in his wardrobe or a second toothbrush in the medicine cabinet, but frankly, that's unlikely. Unless he sells women's clothing or lives with his sister, this man is playing the field – and you're striking out! Get rid of him fast.

2. He doesn't want to get involved

- He is distrustful and secretive and doesn't want you to know him better.
- He fears that a woman will come into his home, rearrange things or clean it up for him, and he doesn't want intrusion into his domain.
- He wants to restrict the intensity of your relationship.
- He's afraid that you will leave personal things that other women will notice.

The Love Codes in any of these patterns of behaviour are quite explicit: he is protecting his privacy to avoid deeper intimacy. When a man's fears are so great that he must maintain an armour of rigid privacy, he is not likely ever to let you come too close. In a healthy relationship a man does not consider a woman's presence in his home to be a sign of invasion or a gesture of conquest.

3. He's totally accommodating

Perhaps his explanation for not inviting you to his house is a totally innocuous one – he may be eager to accommodate you and thinks you are simply more comfortable in your own home. If you suspect that is the case, bring up the subject tactfully – he is a very sensitive and compliant man.

As we have seen, men shape the environment in which they live in very different and very significant ways, and a wealth of Love Codes lie hidden in every room of the house. Try to wangle an early invitation to see his home – even if you just stop by for a quick drink – so that you can glean some information before you get too deeply involved.

6

Is he a product of his culture?

Art is an enigmatic blend of imagination, fantasy and desire. A means of expression unfettered by conventional boundaries, art uses a variety of mediums to make statements that are at once emotional, sensual and informative. A man's cultural preferences – from the books he reads to the art galleries he frequents – reveal his deepest emotional and psychological beliefs, beliefs that have tremendous bearing on his attitudes about love and romance.

Clearly the man who appreciates the complexities of a Wagnerian opera is very different from someone turned on by Madonna or Michael Jackson. He who is engrossed in the latest adventures of a comic book superhero has a very different outlook on the world from someone whose idea of light reading is a six-volume set on Roman civilisation. Cultural preferences can be much more complex or much more subtle, of course. What of the man whose eclectic musical tastes run from arrhythmic jazz to forties musicals? Or the fellow who never sees a film unless it has subtitles, but has a hidden weakness for *The Sound of Music*?

Carefully observe your man's tastes in books, music and film if you want a revealing portrait of what he is *really* like.

DECIPHERING CULTURAL MESSAGES

1. **When you consider his preferences in art, books, television, theatre or film, do you find that he:**

   a. Is fond of one particular subject or theme?
   b. Appreciates a variety of styles and approaches?
   c. Tends to have tastes that are unusual?

2. What sort of entertainment does he like?

a. Light, escapist fare.
b. Cultural activities laden with social messages.
c. A combination of both.

3. In terms of his cultural preferences, is he:

a. Open to new experiences?
b. Rigid and inflexible?
c. Strong, but willing to be swayed on occasion?

4. After seeing a performance together, does he:

a. Insist on delivering critical lectures, as if you lacked his intellectual range?
b. Enjoy analysing and discussing the event?
c. Often agree with your opinion without adding insights of his own?

5. What are his reading habits?

a. He consumes books and magazines voraciously.
b. His reading is confined mostly to the newspaper.
c. He reads books and magazines only in his field of interest.

6. How much television does he watch?

a. More than three hours a night.
b. About an hour a night.
c. Very little, except for special programmes.

7. What is his record, tape and compact disc collection like?

a. A collection of top-40 albums.
b. An eclectic collection of jazz, classical and theatrical music.

c. A treasure trove of rare, outdated or hard-to-find contemporary musical works.

8. How does he respond to a performance he has just seen?

a. Implies that he could have done a better job himself.
b. Assesses both its negative and positive aspects.
c. Offers little opinion one way or the other.

9. Does he feel that:

a. Today's artists will never match the Old Masters?
b. The contemporary art scene is dynamic and superior to the works of the past?
c. There have been great artists throughout history and will surely be others to come?

10. Before deciding to see a new play, does he:

a. Wait to see what the critics have to say?
b. Rely on the opinion of friends?
c. Go and decide for himself?

The Score

Add up the points for each question and check the following answers:

1. a - 2   3. a - 6
   b - 6   b - 2
   c - 4   c - 4

2. a - 2   4. a - 4
   b - 4   b - 6
   c - 6   c - 2

5.	a - 6	8.	a - 4
	b - 2		b - 6
	c - 4		c - 2
6.	a - 2	9.	a - 4
	b - 4		b - 2
	c - 6		c - 6
7.	a - 2	10.	a - 4
	b - 6		b - 2
	c - 4		c - 6

[51-60 points]

This is a man of extraordinarily good taste and excellent critical judgment. The aesthetic dimensions of interpersonal relationships are very important to him, and he seeks women who share his openness to a wide range of cultural influences. He expects sophistication and astute judgment from a lover, but if you are as well-informed as he is, you will find him receptive to your evaluations and suggestions.

[41-50 points]

This man also has refined tastes and a certain finesse, but he holds stubbornly to certain beliefs and preferences. In general, you will find that he is well-informed, emotionally receptive, and reliable. His attitudes towards relationships are like his cultural judgments – generally pretty good but occasionally totally unreasonable. When he stops being reasonable, you must have the confidence to assert your own point of view.

[31-40 points]

From a cultural perspective, this man is neither fish nor fowl. Although he is an expert in some cultural arenas, he knows absolutely nothing about others, yet harbours the illusion that he does. If you become involved in a relationship with this man, you will find it difficult to sway him on certain matters, which can be extremely frustrating.

[20-30 points]
Better look elsewhere if you are seeking a man who is cultivated and elegant in his tastes. This man's sense of aesthetics are determined more by popular whim than by a refined ability to make critical judgments. On the plus side, however, is the fact that this is an easygoing man whose rather lax standards will not be difficult to meet.

A MAN OF LETTERS

Most book collections hold a treasure trove of clues about a man's beliefs, ideas, and values. The subject matter of the volumes, the way in which they are organised and whether they have a well-thumbed or scant-read appearance reveal the nature of his intellectual and cultural interests. More important, careful extrapolation tells you what type of a lover your bookworm will make.

SEAN: A POETIC EXPERIENCE

Marianne: *As soon as I walked into Sean's house I noticed all the volumes of poetry he had. Our first evening together was almost an ethereal experience. He lit candles and read me poems in a rich, mellifluous voice that I found hypnotic. At the end of the evening, I stroked him gently as I said good night and was startled when he shuddered and withdrew his arm.*

I went back to his house a few more times after that, but he never made the slightest effort to be physically affectionate. And I began to notice some other curious things that I had missed before – his volumes of poetry were arranged in strict alphabetical order, for example.

Marianne was initially attracted to Sean's intense and seemingly passionate nature. Unfortunately, her hopes that he would sweep her off her feet were quickly dashed. Sean spent his emotional energy on his poetry and had little left to share with a living, breathing woman. He could speak about the passions of the soul but felt ill-at-ease with passions of the flesh.

On closer analysis, the clues to Sean's rigid behaviour were everywhere. The way in which he arranged his poetry suggests a man whose aesthetic preferences play second fiddle to a passion for orderliness. Perhaps his tightly proscribed habits made it easier for him to control an emotional life that threatened to overwhelm him; regardless, he could not loosen up enough to appreciate Marianne's more casual and freewheeling spirit.

Are his books arranged in a novel way?

Whether a man arranges his books in a fastidious manner or totally haphazardly reveals something about his interest in reading and even more about his approach to loving.

First things first

Often people put the books that are most significant to them within the easiest reach, at the centre of the bookcase. They provide insight into your man's past and give you a sense of his priorities.

As you move away from that focal point, the books fade in importance, representing more superficial interests and attitudes. Pay attention to the books on the periphery. They just might hold a clue about a difficult-to-observe aspect of his personality that could drive you to distraction – or send you to the heights of euphoria.

The subject counts

Another systematic approach is to arrange books by subject. The sign of a true reader who likes to be able to find specific books easily, this man, too, takes good care of possessions that are important to him. A good sign because he is the kind of man who will transfer such a caring approach to you.

Aesthetic appeal

Odder than either an alphabetical or a subject matter arrangement is an arrangement by height. In one library, a man's books were evenly aligned so that each shelf maintained a level effect. The priority for this man is form, not content. A man who uses books for aesthetic effect chooses women superficially too, and is often more concerned about how they look than how they think.

Without rhyme or reason

When you enter his house, the first thing you see are books piled everywhere. Although you may have stumbled across an exceptionally well-read intellectual, you also may be dealing with a man whose mind is in great disarray. Although an individual like this can be very loving, he is likely to forget those special occasions, such as birthdays and anniversaries, that mean so much to you.

Does he get hardbacks or paperbacks?

Hardback

If hardback volumes dominate his collection, you may have found a person who puts a high value on permanence. He values things that last, a trait that extends to his relationships, but he is highly critical and will dismiss a woman whom he judges to be frivolous.

Paperbacks

The man who collects mostly paperbacks is a more adaptable personality. Contemporary in outlook and unlikely to get caught up in long-winded philosophical arguments, the paperback reader is less concerned with appearances, but may be very interested in substance.

Categorically speaking

Study your man's book collection – and most important, note the books that he is currently reading. If one category dominates his library, there is much that can be predicted about his behaviour in a relationship. Here are some of the Love Codes those categories reveal.

Professional and business

A preponderance of career-oriented and investment books indicates a successful man – or one determined to become successful. The fact that he thoroughly researches his subject before making a career move or risking his capital suggests that he is sensible and cautious enough not to fall for get-rich-quick schemes. Similarly, he may need time before he decides that you're a good investment. The only drawback to this go-getter is that he may be too obsessed with his career to make a relationship with you his top priority.

Self-help psychology

A person who avidly reads self-help books is open to change and is interested in learning more about himself in order to improve. Someone who makes personal growth a priority is likely to seek a companion who also believes self-improvement to be important. Rather than sweeping problems in your relationship under the carpet, such a man keeps all channels of communication open. Be on the lookout, however, for the individual who picks up every new pop psychology book that appears on the market – he may be a bit *too* analytical and overly self-involved.

Classics

A man who reads the classics of great literature is generally well-educated, either through formal schooling or self-education, and has cultivated the ability to reason, to think things through, and to solve problems. Those attributes bode well for his ability to tackle the inevitable frictions of a relationship, although his style is overly intellectual for many.

Detective novels

A devotee of Sherlock Holmes, Agatha Christie or Raymond Chandler is generally good at noticing the details others might miss and enjoys exercising skills of logic and reasoning. Becoming involved with such a man could be intriguing, but beware of his strong streak of self-reliance – he may be reluctant to share *all* the intricacies of his life and may often keep you guessing.

Historical novels

Whether it is a historical novel or books on military history, this man is fascinated with the past. He'll want to know all about your previous relationships and may irk you with his notion that history repeats itself. Such men are perceptive though, and often draw intriguing connections between the isolated events of your past. You will also find him particularly forgiving and willing to overlook passing irritations.

Technical manuals

A man whose bookshelves are lined with volumes about machinery, cars, computers, and mathematics is logical and precise. He is more comfortable with the predictable behaviour of machines than with the grey netherworld of emotions, although he may appreciate music and art with a passion. Often men with a technical bent are not emotionally demonstrative, so don't expect to be swept off your feet by this person.

A multifaceted collection

A person whose books cover many different topics is usually curious about life's many facets. Such curiosity often spawns maturity, tolerance and a sophisticated outlook that translates into the flexibility required for a good relationship. A widely-read man has a broad perspective on the world, and his diverse interests make him a complex and intriguing partner.

ROB: WHERE'S THE BEEF?

Lucy: *I was impressed by Rob's collection of expensive art books, which are prominently displayed in his sitting-room. A beautifully bound set of Shakespeare plays in the hallway caught my eye. There was a small collection of rare books and rows of hardcovers, all in excellent condition. I thought to myself, 'at last, a refined and cultured man.' But when I mentioned how much I admired some of the classical writers, he looked as if he'd never heard their names before and seemed to know little about his own collection.*

Here is a man who uses his books to convey an image, rather than to advance his store of knowledge. Appearance, rather than substance, is the force that drives him, a sign that he is deeply insecure and preoccupied with what others think of him. A man who judges books by their cover is likely to apply those same standards to women. Rob can fall madly in love with someone who projects the right image then quickly grow disenchanted when he discovers her flaws. Only a woman who is equally concerned about image will be satisfied with such a self-centred man.

MUSIC IS THE KEY

Music has been called the language of the gods. It is indeed a universal language, but its many dialects express a tremendously varied spectrum of moods and emotions. No one type of music is better or worse than another type, but the sounds a man prefers – and the way in which he listens to those sounds – show important personality traits. Learn how the Love Codes of a man captivated by free-spirited improvisational jazz contrast with those of the classical music devotee, for example, and you will be better able to identify *your* type of man.

BARRY: NOT MUSIC TO HER EARS

Diane: *My ears were ringing as the 'Who' blared incessantly inside Barry's flat, but the sex between us was fast, furious and tremendously exciting. After we had both climaxed, the music really began to get on my nerves. I asked him to lower the volume but he just ignored my suggestion.*
The combination of music and sex had charged the air with energy and we were both too wired to sleep. But Barry didn't respond to my efforts at conversation; he just grooved to the music and held me tight. When I finally reached over to lower the stereo, he blew up at me, 'I just can't deal with a woman who jabbers on when I'm getting into my music' he said.

Barry's capacity to be totally consumed by music initially attracted Diane until she realised that he used music to disconnect himself from others. His passion for music became a barrier behind which he felt safe. The only other way he was able to express himself was in bed, but he could not translate physical intimacy into emotional intimacy. Barry's remarks to Diane and his refusal to turn down the music at her request also show an insensitivity to her feelings that makes a giving relationship impossible.

From adagio to allegro

Primitive percussion sounds intoxicate one man but leave another cold. The man who is moved almost to tears by the haunting melody of an oboe may be utterly indifferent to the power of an electronic bass. Does he have the 'blues'? Maybe that's his outlook on relationships as well as music.

Check out his music collection and note whether the albums, tapes and CD's reflect a fondness for a particular decade, balance contemporary music with older favourites or mix a range of styles. Here are the Love Codes behind particular styles of music:

Classical

A man who appreciates the subtle art of classical music is sensitive to the potential of human achievement. His is a mature sensibility that also values other artistic expressions, such as great paintings, timeless novels and gourmet cuisine. People attuned to the classics are more intro-spective and private than most, and invariably insist on substance along with style. Although your classical music lover may not be given to wild displays of affection, he has deep feelings and the intellect to verbalise them.

Rock

A rock music aficionado tends to be more energetic and freer in his lifestyle than most men. Young at heart, tuned into contemporary trends and a little hedonistic, he may turn to the lyrics of his favourite rock musicians to justify his attitudes towards sex, work, responsibility and freedom. If you share this man's obsession with rock and roll, you may just find that you are on the same wavelength.

Folk music

A hard-core group of sensitive folk out there is concerned with social issues and passionately committed to improving the environment, eliminating nuclear weapons and pro-moting human rights. They see music as a tool to help save the world and value the ideas contained in the lyrics. If you are a woman devoted to good causes, the folkie can be a splendid choice – he is sincere, comfortable with himself and appreciative of an honest and open relationship. Don't expect great wealth, though. These men aren't driven by the kind of ambition that translates into overwhelming financial success.

Jazz

Jazz enthusiasts are an eclectic collection of nonconformists who defy ready analysis. Although the underlying structure of jazz requires well-disciplined thinking, the brilliance of the music relies on improvisation and experimentation. Independence, a sense of adventure, a resistance to repetitive patterns and a determination to do things his way are his hallmarks.

Here is a multifaceted individual guaranteed to give the woman in his life a one-of-a-kind experience. But be prepared, however, for the ups and downs of his fascinating, contradictory character, which will always remain unpredictable and uncontrollable.

Opera

The finest opera is laden with pomp and ceremony, and the man who cultivates a taste for this high art form has great respect for tradition and values predictability and appropriateness. In all manner of personal conduct and social interaction, he proceeds with style and taste. Be forewarned: an opera lover expects perfection, but when he sees what he likes, his enthusiasm is boundless. If you can tolerate a certain rigidity of thought, this man can offer you tremendous emotional rewards.

Top 40

Basically romantic and easygoing, this man does not like to engage in endless introspective dialogue about relationships, preferring to see them evolve at their own relaxed pace. He does, however, hold the rather romantic notion that love with the right person will solve just about all of life's problems. Unfortunately, this fantasy makes it easier for him to walk away instead of confronting and dealing with tensions between you.

Country and western

Here's a man who is in love with love and committed to pursuing close relationships but not always very successful at it. He is capable of experiencing deep emotion and talks as honestly about poverty, rejection and hardship as he does about successful conquests and rewarding relationships. One of the real charms of the country-western buff is that he is unselfconscious and willing to act silly, yet never compromises his self-respect.

Blues

This man treats life as an emotional, rather than an intellectual, experience. Warm and communicative, he empathises with the struggles of others, especially in the realm of romance. He is melancholy, but not cynical, about love and is willing to take emotional risks, even if there is a chance of being rejected.

Hollywood musicals

Romantic and sensitive, this man has a nostalgic feeling for bygone days and a rather corny way with words. But he deliberates carefully before talking and means every word he says so you'd better watch your own language and avoid speaking carelessly. In a relationship the musical addict tends to be a bit overly emotional, and prone to dramatic bursts of emotion, but it is all in the interest of staving off the familiar and the boring.

Gospel

Preoccupied with religious values, his faith plays a significant part in his life and he seeks a woman who shares his religious beliefs. If your faith is comparable to his, you will find him a trustworthy and dedicated family man. But if your spiritual values differ significantly, a meaningful long-term relationship is unlikely to develop.

IS HE A WORK OF ART?

The art a man admires and chooses to display on his walls contains information about his self-image and his perspective on the world. Whether it is a photograph, a reproduction, or an original painting, we select art because it strikes a responsive chord in us and somehow helps to communicate our view of the world. In order to determine the Love Codes buried in a man's choices, look around his home and try to determine the statement that each piece of art makes.

Questionnaire: The curator of the house

Answer each of the following questions with: All, Many, Some, Few or None.

1. Does he display portraits of family and friends?
2. Are there sexual images in the pictures he displays?
3. Are the pictures warm and inviting rather than cold and impersonal?
4. Is there an element of the comical or whimsical?
5. Do you find his art collection appealing?
6. Are the images tranquil rather than violent or threatening?
7. Are the facial and bodily features attractive rather than distorted or ugly?
8. Is there an eclectic balance of pictures rather than a collection representing only one style?
9. Do the works reflect dreams as opposed to nightmares?
10. Do his pictures tend to be bright and colourful rather than dark and foreboding?

The score

Tally up your score with the following points: All = 4 points; Many = 3 points; Some = 2 points; Few = 1 point; None = 0 points.

[31-40 points]
A warm, positive person with a bright and optimistic attitude towards life has selected this art. Fundamentally life-affirming, you can expect him to be loving and generous in a relationship. No emotional storms cloud his mind; no dark, lingering anger is likely to explode at any moment. Here is that rare individual who appreciates the beauty life has to offer, and finds much to praise – and little to criticize – in the woman he loves.

[21-30 points]
Basically a positive and caring individual, this man has a few unresolved emotional dilemmas that add a dimension of tantalizing complexity many women find attractive. He often deliberately uses his art to make a social or political statement, and if you agree with his outlook, he is a good bet as a romantic partner.

[11-20 points]
There are multifaceted dimensions to this complex personality. His artwork reveals a personality schism in which he is sometimes bright, cheerful and optimistic, and other times depressed and negative. There is some unresolved anger boiling inside this man, and if you become involved, you may find him to be a moody mystery. One day he'll surprise you with flowers, the next day say something cruel and uncaring. It is a challenge to learn how to respond to this man who is well-meaning, but in conflict.

[0-10 points]
By almost any measure, this individual is alienated and distant from emotional interaction. Inclined to see only the worst in people, he is highly suspicious and reclusive by nature. There will be far more pain and misery than compassion in this relationship and it is best to stay clear.

Different strokes

Here's a brief analysis of some specific painting styles and an explanation of the Love Codes they project:

Abstract

As enigmatic to their owners as they are to viewers, abstract paintings deliberately lend an air of mystery to a home. A man who displays such imagery is one who believes that people are entitled to interpret reality in any way they see fit. Although he may be intrigued by life's unanswered questions, he's not concerned with arriving at firm answers. On the plus side, a man attached to abstract art rarely approaches a relationship with hard-and-fast rules of appropriate behaviour. But don't expect this man to provide a clear definition of where you stand; after all, hiding his true feelings is part of the fun.

Old masters

Reproductions, one assumes, but nonetheless when you spot a Da Vinci or Rembrandt hanging on the wall, you've found a man with some old-fashioned values. Conservative in lifestyle, but passionate about genius, this is a man who believes the finer things in life must withstand the test of time. There is an elegance to everything he does and despite his reserve and controlled manner, you may appreciate his romantic style. If you pride yourself on being a woman who acts like a lady, be prepared to share candlelit dinners with this gentleman.

Impressionism

Beneath those light-dappled bursts of colour and pointillistic landscapes are layers of meaning waiting to be unwrapped. The man who displays impressionist art tends to be analytical, a shrewd observer who probes beneath appearances and discovers depths hidden to the casual onlooker. Because he will scrutinise every detail in order to see to the core of an issue, this man is a shrewd judge of human nature. In a relationship he is likely to be a good listener and a perceptive observer who is willing to wait for a woman to open up to him.

Realist

Art is simply a way to state facts, according to the collector of realist works, who likes his paintings to be clear, direct, and accessible. Translate those qualities into his dealings with people, and you've found a man who wants to know where people stand, what they want and who they want it from. If his literalism seems to lack a touch of imagination, at least he will present no unpleasant surprises, nor will his expectations of you be unrealistic!

Avant-garde

A restless probing spirit, this man is constantly on the prowl for dramatic new experiences and adventures. Not content merely to read about the latest trends, he's part of what fuels their success. He's a risk-taker, always in pursuit of new styles – traditional values don't hold much importance to him – and he'll introduce you to worlds you never even knew existed. If the cutting edge excites you, too, you can help make this relationship a hot one.

Primitive

The collector of primitive art is drawn to adventure of a very different sort. A lover of rituals and symbolism, he will travel to exotic and far-flung places in search of local colour and mystery. Driven by his own set of myths about noble savages and tribal harmony, he tends to romanticise non-Western ways. You may have to give up some creature comforts to follow this man, but if you don't have all the conventional expectations of the urban upwardly mobile, he could open your eyes to new worlds.

GIVING HIM A SCREEN TEST

Cinema is one of the most popular forms of culture today, and films are an important measure of compatibility. Whether you prefer the excitement of the big screen or the intimacy of the VCR, it won't be long before you discover whether or not you and your man enjoy the same types of films. Equally important, you'll soon learn how well the two of you can discuss and evaluate the films you see together.

Today's films appeal to almost every taste imaginable, from the obscurely artistic to the mesmerisingly violent. Because each one makes a statement about values that prompts an emotional reaction from the viewer, you can learn a lot about a man's Love Codes from his film preferences.

LOUIS: THE FOREIGN FILM PEDANT

Sophie: *Louis and I were introduced at a publishing party and he invited me to see a revival of a Bergman film. After we saw the film, he took great pains to explain the significance of each scene in detail, including an analysis of the movements made by the camera.*

In the course of the next month we saw the latest Wenders movie, a Japanese film that I didn't understand, and something political from South America. After he dragged me to a three and a half hour picture from Rumania I finally blew my top and said the next film we saw had to be in English. He looked at me with sheer horror and proceeded to deliver a lecture about the superficiality of American movies.

Louis's approach to Sophie was far more patronising than enlightening. By deliberately dominating their post-film discussions, he made genuine dialogue impossible. A man who tries to dazzle others with his insights and intellect is only spotlighting his own lack of confidence.

Louis's insistence on selecting films that *he* wanted to see, regardless of Sophie's preferences, is a patent display of selfishness and suggests that he may need total control over any situation, which is hardly grist for an egalitarian relationship. This is a man who will only satisfy a woman willing to acknowledge his superior intelligence, cultural sophistication and elitist attitude.

What are your man's preferences?

Foreign

Of course, not all foreign film enthusiasts are like Louis. A passion for foreign films also suggests erudition and a broad vision of the world. Don't be intimidated by a man's enthusiasm for foreign movies. If there is mutual respect in your relationship, you can learn from him without allowing him to dominate. Perhaps you can strike a pact, alternating between foreign and American or English films. If he respects your choices, he'll think that's a fair deal; if not, good riddance?

Femme fatales

The worlds inhabited by Betty Grable, Joan Crawford and Lauren Bacall have long past, but it is not hard to find the man who still honours their memory. They see classic films of the 1930s, 1940s and 1950s over and over again and often feel dissatisfied with contemporary mores – and the women the times have spawned. Some men who watch these films to the exclusion of other genres often feel like misfits. Although their manners may be refreshingly old-fashioned, they are often unrealistic about their relationships, approaching them through the distorted lens of a distant era.

Action/adventure

A man enamoured of such films usually admires the strength and resourcefulness of their male stars. At bottom is usually a fear of his own impotence, which he will try to hide beneath a blustery, macho exterior. The occasional escape into the fantasy world of the action/adventure movie is a reasonable release, but an obsession with such films to the exclusion of all others reflects deep frustration. Such a man may be preoccupied with attempting to prove his 'manhood' to you.

Documentary

Whether it is a film about racism in South Africa or the lives of Appalachian coal miners, the man who regularly attends documentaries is usually serious, socially conscious and concerned about the welfare of others. Films are no means of release to this man; rather, they are a tool that enables him to learn more about the world around him. If you share his sensibilities and concerns, there's a good bet here, but don't expect too much frippery from him. He takes life seriously and is looking for a woman who does, too. He makes firm commitments and sees them through.

Westerns

The plot of most Westerns is built around a simplistic portrayal of good against evil. Because the moral questions raised are answered clearly and without ambivalence, these films appeal to solid, unpretentious men. You'll find the Western enthusiast to be practical and to have both feet solidly on the ground, but don't expect him to cope with the complex issues that most contemporary films tackle. Such a man is strong-willed and a bit traditional in his outlook, but he knows the rules of proper behaviour in a relationship and he'll fight for the woman he loves.

Horror

The need to test one's strength and courage is quite apparent in the man who feels compelled to see one horror film after another. He has a rather adolescent attitude, and

you'll find that he has a hard time relaxing with you, because he feels obliged to prove he's not scared of you, a relationship, or anything.

Another type of man, though fewer in number, identifies with the victim. He feels terrible things have been done to him by life. For this reason, he's masking a great deal of anger and, in relationships, he may view himself as the innocent victim of evil intent. See if he describes the women in his past as being monsters.

Comedy

The lover of comedy films is fortunate in possessing a good sense of humour, which can be vital to the survival of any involvement. He generally enjoys life and is optimistic, but it may be hard for him to discuss serious emotions. Although his feelings run deep, he sometimes conceals them by infusing his conversations with one-liners and humorous asides. You have to be able to deflect these in order to discover the sweet and sensitive person underneath.

Science fiction

This man is an idealist with a utopian vision of the future. If you become involved with him, you'll open yourself up to a person who likes to try new things and is particularly fascinated by the latest technical gadgets. Never dismiss this man's favourite films as fantasy – true, he may cope with the problems of the present by escaping into the future, but he is also sensitive and profoundly concerned with building a better tomorrow.

We have seen how cultural preferences provide an important glimpse at a man's emotional makeup. Because he has an almost infinite collection of music, works of art, books and films to choose from, his selections are a clear expression of his personality and his inclinations in a relationship. Be particularly certain to scrutinise any conflicts between his tastes – for example, the man who likes both Old Master paintings and rock-and-roll music is a complex individual who can not be readily pigeonholed, but may well be worth a closer look.

7

His work and your union

There is a clear but complex connection between the way a man treats his professional colleagues and his friends and the way in which he will treat you. Although he often responds to a lover with a gentleness that he does not exhibit at work, it is rare for a man to undergo a complete transformation between his public and his private life.

There are exceptions, of course. A man who is known to be very aggressive and critical with his employees is said to be a real pussycat with his domineering wife; a man who is docile and acquiescent with friends may be more confident in asserting himself at home with his wife and children. Don't count on it though, and don't delude yourself by creating dreams based on false hopes. If a man is capable of a particular emotional reaction – whether it is anger, love or jealousy – with even one person, the proper stimulus can evoke the same reaction again. The greatest mistake a woman can make is to believe that she can change a man's basic personality.

A LABOUR OF LOVE

Research has shown that people choose their jobs to meet a range of psychological, intellectual and creative needs. Men who are most satisfied with their work are in positions appropriate to their personality makeup. These are the men with a positive and self-confident outlook on life and they tend to be tolerant towards others and a pleasure to be with.

Men who are dissatisfied with their lot in life are often jealous and resentful of anyone who is happy, and they seek scapegoats for ther disappointments. Such men will resent your optimistic perspective and make your life uncomfortable.

The answers to the following questions will help you identify the category into which your man falls.

IS HIS JOB WORKING FOR HIM?

Answer the following questions with, Always, Frequently, Occasionally, Seldom, or Never.

1.   Does he blame others for his failures at work?
2.   Does he value his own achievements regardless of the recognition he receives?
3.   Is he more likely to criticize, rather than praise, the performance of his colleagues?
4.   Is he co-operative, instead of suspicious, when management suggest a change in routine?
5.   Does he feel jealous in the presence of other men, believing that they are more successful than he?
6.   Does he seek to acquire the knowledge and expertise that will advance his career?
7.   Is he content to relate only to people in his field, rather than expand his horizons?
8.   Does he meet all his work deadlines?
9.   Does he make work commitments that he can't fulfill?
10. Does he view criticism as a valuable tool that can help improve his job performance, rather than as a personal attack?
11. Does he seek new acquaintances primarily on the basis of what they can do for him?
12. Does he have a clear-cut agenda for achieving success through a series of well-planned steps?
13. Does he spend a lot of time lamenting lost opportunities and mistakes?
14. Does he appear to enjoy his job and speak about it with enthusiasm?
15. Is he highly competitive, determined to win at any cost?
16. Is he capable of striking a balance between work and his personal life?
17. Does he feel that he is in a rut, discouraged by his prospects but unable to do anything about them?

18. Does he tend to socialize with his co-workers?
19. Is he constantly annoyed or irritated by situations at work?
20. Does he believe that his job enables him to make the most of his creative and personal potential?

The score

For questions with *even* numbers, score as follows: Always = 4 points; Frequently = 3 points; Occasionally = 2 points; Seldom = 1 point; Never = 0 points.

For questions with *odd* numbers, score as follows: Always = 0 points; Frequently = 1 point; Occasionally = 2 points; Seldom = 3 points; Never = 4 points.

[61-80 points]
Even more than having a positive outlook on his career, this man has the self-assurance and selflessness that signals a secure and motivated personality. He works well with others and is as eager to find a compatible relationship as he is to perform well on the job. And when he does find it, he will use his strength and resourcefulness to make it work.

[41-60 points]
This man is basically satisfied with his career, but he also harbours a certain degree of restlessness. From time to time he thinks that somewhere, perhaps, life has a little more to offer him. If he is able to express his reservations constructively, he is a good bet for an emotional involvement because he's aware of both the positive and negative aspects of his situation. Expect him to be able to make a solid emotional commitment.

[21-40 points]
This man has some definite reservations about the direction in which his life is moving. Dissatisfied with a career that

provides more frustrations than rewards, he tends to view his job as a way to survive rather than a source of fulfillment. Because he does not experience much pleasure from his work, he may expect a relationship to satisfy all his emotional needs. Beware a tendency to be demanding and critical.

[0-20 points]
Almost totally alienated from his job, this man is angry and hostile, yet feels powerless to make real changes. He is caught in the grip of forces he cannot control, and indeed feels resentful of, and makes a very poor choice as a potential mate.

HIS ROLE IN THE WORKPLACE

One man prefers a job without heavy responsibilities so that he can leave it behind when the day is over. Another wants to devote himself to his career with passionate commitment. Some men work alone, others thrive only in groups; some seek recognition in high-visibility fields, others work only for personal satisfaction.

Here are the Love Codes behind the way in which a man earns his daily bread and relates to the co-workers around him.

Boss Man

Most people who run their own businesses owe their success to hard work, shrewd politicking and sheer talent. A man in charge may be a bit arrogant, believing himself smarter than anyone around him and resentful about ceding control. Independent, strong willed and stubborn, he is equipped to handle responsibility and knows how to behave in a position of authority.

It can be very difficult for the boss to take off that authoritative hat when he leaves the office, a trait that has its pros and cons in a relationship. This man is a good problem solver who accepts the necessity for hard work and he is a steady source of support in a crisis. The boss is used to giving orders, however, in the home as well as at work, and he expects his opinions to be respected. Many bosses are drawn to passive women, which is why women who abhor decision making may find the 'bossy' man a godsend. More assertive women may find a relationship with this man a constant struggle.

Just a Job

The rank-and-file employee stands in marked contrast to the boss. He detests being in charge, does not want to take responsibility for others, and prefers the security of a

127

structured role and a regular wage. This is the perfect man for a woman who likes to take over. He is happy to bring home his wage packet and let her pay the bills, make social arrangements and generally organise their lives.

A man who is content to be a rank-and-file employee has chosen a relaxed and modest lifestyle over the rat race. If you are attracted to him because he's a laid-back, dependable family man, don't be surprised to discover that he's not terribly ambitious either on the job or in the home. As always, it is important to be realistic about what you really want.

Room at The Top

A man who has risen to the top ranks of a large company has learned to be a team player, to share responsibility and to adapt to the needs of others – when they fit into his game plan. He is goal-oriented, ambitious and focused on tangible achievements. There is not much room for spontaneity in this man's life and he doesn't welcome unexpected change, but his consistent, predictable and straightforward approach makes many women feel secure.

Remember, though, that a top manager tends to take close personal ties for granted. Like the secretarial support staff he relies too heavily on, he sees close friends and family as indispensable, but often forgets to give them the tender, loving care they require. From time to time, you will have to shake his complacency and remind him of your importance in his life. Try mysteriously absenting yourself for one day a week and see how he feels about that.

On His Own

Although there is no one to tell him when to come to work or how to do his job, the man who works for himself, whether as a freelance writer or as a commission salesman, has a great deal of discipline and a strong sense of responsibility. He values independence more than security and is accustomed to being his own man, answering neither to bosses nor to employees.

A relationship with a self-employed man can be exciting, spontaneous and unpredictable. He genuinely believes in egalitarian partnerships and will give you as much freedom as he demands back. Although this man doesn't make commitments readily, he sticks to the ones he chooses. He's an ideal partner for the woman who desires independence and assumes responsibility for herself. If you need a strong sense of stability, though, better look elsewhere.

Professionally Speaking

Whether he is a lawyer, a doctor, or an architect, the professional man is often hotly pursued by women because he combines some of the best qualities of each of the men described previously. He has the confidence and independence to be a boss and the ability of a rank-and-file employee to acquiesce to ethical and legal codes of conduct.

Alas, the professional man tends to be somewhat impressed by his own importance. Because society endows him with high status and respects his authority, he often develops an attitude of superiority to others. You may have to struggle to penetrate his thick skin and uncover the vulnerability below. A man who thinks that he is a great catch for a lucky woman is often too arrogant to accept criticism or acknowledge any need to change. But if you're satisfied with him just the way he is, then you may indeed have a great catch!

Unemployed: Down or Out?

Many people are unemployed at some stage in their life for very legitimate reasons, and you'll need to know more about your man's history before making any generalisations based on his job status. Perhaps he is pursuing a creative or entrepreneurial career that has not yet got off the ground. He could be independently wealthy or chronically lazy, determined to find an appropriate outlet for his talents or unrealistic about his options for the future.

Being unemployed does not have to mean being unproductive and you can learn a lot about your man by asking these questions about his attitude:

- Does he have a positive outlook or is he morose and negative?
- Does he blame others for his predicament?
- Is he open to new and unexpected opportunities?
- Is he pursuing occupational leads?
- How does he spend his free time?

Although no one has a guarantee of finding an ideal job, a man who remains hopeful, patient and positive is far more likely to come out on top of any situation. Someone who is depressed handicaps himself and turns off those around him. Your reactions during this period in his life will reveal as much about your ability to handle adversity as about his. They will also help to gauge the extent of your respect and devotion to this man.

The jobs described here, and many others, require a unique set of skills and reveal a great deal about your man's personality and his interest in a relationship. Some jobs, such as sales, are mostly people-oriented, and salesmen know how to put others at ease, which can be a real plus in a relationship. Or a job may force a man to deal with many underlings – the way he treats them reveals a lot about his respect for others, including you. By learning as much as you can about the type of work he does and how he does it, you will understand yet another important dimension of his personality.

8

The company he keeps

Most of us try to make a good impression when we meet someone new, especially in the early stages of courting. But we'll let down our guard with friends, especially people we know well. Matching a man's interactions with those who know him best and listening to what others say about him are thus likely to be very revealing. Forge ahead if they describe him as a loyal friend and a decent human being. Use caution if they jokingly call him a real pain but say they love him anyway – try to find out if there is more joke or more truth in their banter.

Analyse the anecdotes they tell about him. Is he the guy who saved the day by rounding up oversized tents when it rained for the family picnic? Or was he the one thrown out of a posh restaurant when he became drunk and disorderly? Is he thought of as someone who can be counted on in a jam or as someone who creates those jams?

WILL HE BE A FRIEND TO YOU?

The first of the following statements applies to men who are reliable, friendly, outgoing and sincere. The statement in parentheses is the opposite extreme and applies to men who are withdrawn, antisocial and insecure. On a scale of 5 to 0, where a score of 5 means the first statement is 100 per cent applicable, judge where he falls between the polar opposites.

1. He has welcomed you into his social world. (The opposite: He fails to introduce you to anybody.)
2. He calls his friends often. (The opposite: His friends have to pursue him.)

3. His friends believe him to be a man who always comes to help in a crisis. (The opposite: He never extends himself to help others.)
4. He has friends of both sexes. (The opposite: All his friends are of one sex.)
5. He genuinely enjoys listening to someone else relate a story. (The opposite: He always tries to top the stories he hears.)
6. His pleasure in the accomplishments of his friends is evident and sincere. (The opposite: He is jealous of the achievements of others.)
7. He is modest about his own success. (The opposite: He inflates the importance of his achievements.)
8. He looks forward to parties. (The opposite: He attends parties purely out of a sense of obligation.)
9. He is very good at remembering names and faces. (The opposite: He rarely remembers the names of those he has met on previous occasions.)
10. He is always prompt for appointments. (The opposite: He is always late.)
11. He goes out of his way to help family or friends in trouble. (The opposite: His family and friends have to beg him for assistance.)
12. He tries to see events from other people's perspective. (The opposite: He passes judgement on others without bothering to understand their point of view.)
13. He is genuinely close to a number of people. (The opposite: All his relationships are casual and transitory.)
14. Many of his friendships extend back at least four or five years. (The opposite: Most of his friendships are of recent vintage.)
15. He usually gives people the benefit of the doubt. (The opposite: He is quick to condemn others.)
16. He uses his friends as a sounding board when he experiences setbacks. (The opposite: He suffers his disappointments in silence.)

17. When plans change, he can make the transition with a minimum of effort. (The opposite: He fusses endlessly about disruptions in his plans.)
18. He periodically hosts dinner or cocktail parties. (The opposite: He is the eternal guest.)
19. He sends cards or gifts to friends to commemorate holidays, birthdays and anniversaries. (The opposite: He never remembers the special occasions of those close to him.)
20. He tries to get together with friends regularly. (The opposite: He seems indifferent to seeing his friends.)

The Score

Add up the points and read what your score means below:

[81 – 100 points]
This man is refreshingly loyal, empathetic and sincere. He makes an effort to stay in touch with many people, goes out of his way for his friends, and takes care of those close to him in time of need. These are rare attributes indeed in self-centred and narcissistic times, and his strong sense of values makes him a fine relationship catch. He is secure enough to allow you to blossom.

[61 – 80 points]
This man is enthusiastic and positive about life and generous and gregarious in a love relationship. He values his friendships and you can expect him to be very attentive and concerned with your well-being. Despite the value he places on friendship and love, however, there are a number of other priorities in his life.

[41 – 60 points]
This person takes a rigidly egalitarian view towards relationships – he is willing to give just what he receives, no more and no less. Unless he is sure you will respond to his affections with equal enthusiasm, he is not likely to be overly demonstrative. Expect your involvement with this man to evolve slowly and cautiously.

[21 – 40 points]
This man is something of a loner and you will have to make a concerted effort to keep your relationship going. It is difficult for him to get close to others because of the hard-to-penetrate defensive shields that he has erected. Even the most determined woman won't be able to penetrate all his barriers or force him to respond with as much depth of feeling as she would like.

[0 – 20 points]
Stay away! This man borders on being completely anti-social, making little or no effort to extend himself to others. Indeed he seems to be wrapped so tightly in his emotional shell that he is virtually unresponsive. This is a clear sign that he doesn't care for himself enough to think he is worthy of even the most rudimentary contacts with others.

HOW WELL DOES HE SHARE?

One of the questions that always arises when a couple first get involved is how to relate to each other's friends. Some couples adopt the other's chums wholesale and plan all social activities as a unit. Others insist on maintaining some independent friendships outside their primary love relationship. There are no rules to follow on this issue, but the choice a man makes tells you how he will treat you in a relationship.

RICK: SHARE AND SHARE ALIKE

Fay: *Being with Rick opened up a whole new world to me. He was an actor who knew all kinds of show-business people I would never have the opportunity to meet as a teacher in primary school. I learned a lot from them and it also helped me understand Rick better.*

A man who wants to share his friends demonstrates a generosity of spirit and a genuine respect for you. Proud of the friendships he has developed over the years and excited about your fledging relationship, he is open enough to invite you to share an important part of his life. Rick clearly understands the importance of close connections, whether they are good friends or significant lovers.

Similarly, a man who really cares for you will want to get to know your friends better. We *should* judge each other by the company we keep, and a man will understand you better if he shares that part of your life, at least some of the time.

SIMON: NEVER THE TWAIN SHALL MEET

Sheila: *Simon socialised with a lot of people, but he never invited me to go out with them. He divided his weekend so that we would spend one night together and he would go out alone with his friends on the other night. Although we had been seeing each other for six months, I had never even met his best friend. I really resented being kept in one small compartment of his life.*

Although a man is certainly entitled to spend time alone with his friends, Simon's refusal to introduce Sheila to important people in his life suggests that he is not totally committed to their relationship, and therefore does not want to mingle it with the more permanent elements in his life. His reluctance to share his friends indicates a selfish streak, as well. Be prepared to bicker about sharing expenses and household chores, too.

In a similar vein, some men resent the time or emotional energy that a woman devotes to anyone besides him. By couching his resentment towards your friends in terms that emphasise his love for you, ('But, Diana, don't you *want* to spend as much time together as we can?') a man can be deliberately manipulative. Don't be fooled, though – true love is expansive, not restricting, and his resentment is no sign of love.

GRAHAM: NOT A FRIEND IN THE WORLD

Judy: *It really bothered me that Graham had no friends of his own and no interest in my friends either. I had so many friends, and I thought there was something wrong with him. I hated leaving the house and seeing him sit on the couch so forlorn – like a lost puppy dog. And he certainly did his best to make me feel guilty about leaving him alone. That was the worst part of it – he was so dependent on me because he had no one else to turn to.*

A man's lack of male friends is a source of irritation and unhappiness to many women. Women are often initially attracted to a man who is emotionally dependent because he is reassuring and attentive early in their meetings – often when she feels uncertain and eager for commitment. Only later, when she feels more secure and ready to resume her 'normal' pattern, will she recognise that this loving and responsive puppy dog is really an albatross.

Be warned that a man without friends usually finds it very difficult to be close to others and does not readily share his feelings. Although he will rely on you to satisfy his emotional needs, it may be difficult to drag him from the shell in which he has encased his emotional self.

GARRY: YOUR FRIENDS ARE HIS FRIENDS

Rhonda: *It was a good thing that Garry didn't have any friends of his own, because I am so involved with mine that I insist on spending a lot of time with them. It has worked out perfectly because he is willing to adopt all my friends as his own.*

For emotional and cultural reasons, many men simply do not have friends with whom they can share confidences. Others feel they have to cut ties with their past when they become involved with a woman. But when a man is without friends because of circumstance, rather than because he is emotionally withdrawn, he will happily embrace your friends. In the process he makes a significant statement about your importance in his life. Kudos for the man who accepts and respects you and seeks intimate bonding by sharing your life.

Keeping Your Friends to Yourself

Not all women are grateful for a man who is eager to share her friends. Perhaps you are reluctant to make that final commitment to your lover or do not respect him quite enough to go public with him. Or, you may feel a bit insecure about your relationship and prefer to be the focus of *all* his attentions. Better take a close look at your own motives.

A man's own friendships – and his response to yours – can give you strong hints about his ability to sustain relationships, the kinds of emotional connections he values and, ultimately, about your compatibility. Keep in mind, though, that men and women often have different attitudes about the role of friendship in their lives. Male friendships traditionally focus more on shared activities and interests and less on shared feelings and personal revelations. As long as they do not become an excuse to avoid emotional exploration, those types of bonds can be just as meaningful.

9

Partying

Throughout this book we have discussed many personality traits that can clearly be categorized as either desirable or undesirable – selfishness, generosity, hostility and affection, for example. But there are also many forms of social behaviour that are neither good nor bad, only inappropriate for some people. In these cases, a man's desirability as a partner depends on *your* personality and needs.

ONE WOMAN'S MEAT . . .

In the case studies that follow, the differing reactions of two women to the same man show that the man who is one woman's meat can be a poison for another.

JACK: THE LIFE OF THE PARTY

Yvette: *Jack is a friendly and gregarious man and he is known as the life and soul of the party. He makes everyone feel at ease, but the truth is that I never enjoy being with him in a big crowd. As soon as we get to a party, he immediately takes over and totally obscures me. He'll tell these god-awful salesman jokes filled with sexual innuendos. I am sometimes embarrassed to be with him.*

Julia: *I really thrive on going to parties with Jack. People flock to him because he is funny and enthusiastic and open. He blazes the trail for us to meet everyone at the party. I'm a little shy and it certainly is convenient to have such a ready entrée into a crowd of strangers.*

A man who is the centre of the party thrives on being the centre of attention and is often a genuine crowd-pleaser. The need to dominate a group, however, can also indicate a

141

person who is far from confident about himself. By the same token, his sexually-laden humour could signal a level of discomfort with the real thing – or it could mean that he's a man to whom sex is particularly important.

Yvette is dismayed and put off by Jack's behaviour and resents playing second fiddle to him. She needs to find the man who is more reserved and willing to let her share the limelight. Julia, on the other hand, profits from all the attention Jack receives. Not one who seeks attention herself, she thrives in his reflected glory.

JOE: THE MAN'S MAN

Monica: *When I go to Joe's house it is like attending an ongoing bachelor party. He'll invite the lads over to watch football and cricket and, like most men, they seldom clean up after themselves. When they aren't watching sports together, they all go off on shooting and fishing expeditions, leaving me*

feeling lonely and irritated. Joe is always very affectionate, but I am unhappy that we have so little time alone together.

Sally: *There was a time when I thought that Joe must be gay because he seemed to want to spend all his time with his male friends. He works with men, spends his evenings with men, takes holidays with men. He never even talks to women at parties – instead I'll spot him in a corner sharing a laugh with the usual gang of lads.*

I really value my independence and need space and time to pursue my own interests, so my relationship with Joe has been perfect. I don't have to worry that he is with another woman and, when we are together, he is very affectionate. We genuinely enjoy each other's company but we spend a lot of time apart.

Men like Joe are accustomed to the company of men and share a camaraderie with them that they simply cannot replicate with women. Although Joe is genuinely affectionate and appreciates loyalty, his social needs are largely satisfied by his colleagues at work and his friends at home. When he does crave the warmth that only a woman can provide, he is grateful – if you will accept him on his terms.

Monica, who is looking for a relationship in which she can spend most of her spare time with the man she loves, feels anger and frustration with Joe. Sally, however, finds exactly what she needs with him. Many independent women find it highly advantageous to be involved with a 'man's man' because they have the security of commitment without the pressure of confinement.

ROGER: FLIRTATIOUS BUT NOT FICKLE

Rita: *I know that Roger is a big flirt, but frankly I thrive on the fact that he's attractive to every woman who meets him. It's an ego trip, I admit, but I get a kick from the envy of other women. When a woman is really coming on strong to him, I get a pang of insecurity but I realize that Roger flirts because he needs to be reassured about his desirability.*

Judy: *I stopped seeing Roger after just a few dates because of his flirtatious behaviour. He kept assuring me that he was genuinely interested in pursuing a relationship, but he also wanted every woman in the room to pay attention to him. After a while, I decided I wanted someone who considered me woman enough.*

It takes a very confident woman to be comfortable with a ladies' man, but Rita is right – Roger's compulsive flirtation is a compensation for his feelings of inadequacy, not a search for another woman. A man who is genuinely fond of women tends to have a lot of close female friends and he can be a warm and communicative partner to someone special. If you're at peace with the green-eyed monster of jealousy, all signals are go here.

Insecure women need to beware, however. Watching her man flirt in a crowd sent shivers through Judy, and she could never relax when she was out with Roger or he was out alone. Although he frequently reassured her of the depth of his feelings, he never stopped flirting because he needed continual reassurance. Second thoughts are in order for a woman who seeks a man's undivided attention.

SIMON: NO FLASH BUT A LOT OF SUBSTANCE

Maxine: *Simon is a terrific bloke but I certainly didn't realize it when friends introduced us at a party. He was cordial but seemed terribly ill at ease. I would never have gone out with him except that our mutual friends kept telling me what a great guy he was. When we finally got together for dinner, I was amazed at how relaxed and interesting he turned out to be.*

Iris: *Simon certainly commands a lot of respect among the people who know him best, but I can't help thinking he's a little dull. I was reluctant to go out with him the first time, and my friends practically had to twist my arm to convince me to give him a second chance. I'm sure he's a genuinely decent person but I like a man with some fire, someone that other people notice. A shrinking violet just isn't my scene.*

Men who seem quiet may actually be very shy, able to emerge from their shells only in social settings in which they feel comfortable and accepted. Some men are particularly shy with women but very much at ease with male friends or colleagues; others are able to relax with outgoing women who can initiate the conversation and do not have hard-and-fast definitions of proper social skills.

Women often fail to measure the true depths of bashful men who may offer more substance and commitment than a more glamorous personality. In a relaxed one-to-one situation, Maxine was pleasantly surprised by Simon's attributes. Iris, however, knew that she wanted a man with a lot more dazzle and spark than Simon. She was right to stop seeing him. After all, there is no point in continuing an unsatisfying relationship. Many unhappy marriages are the result of such inertia.

MATTHEW: MR PRIVATE

Kate: *Matthew is always so mysterious and reserved about what he does and who he does it with that it adds to the excitement of our being together. Our relationship is built on the basis of mutual respect for each other's privacy. I really appreciate the space he gives me, and I try to give him the same. I've always been uncomfortable about having to account for my whereabouts.*

Mary: *Matthew's insistence on his privacy leaves me feeling intrusive if I ask even the most casual question, such as where he had lunch. I like a little breathing space myself, but this man doesn't know the meaning of intimacy. He never shares his feelings with me and I know very little about the people or activities that keep him occupied. When we get together we are like two people who have no existence outside of each other!*

People who rigorously guard their privacy tend to be vulnerable and suspicious of the motives of others.

Unconsciously, they feel that any information they volunteer can be used against them. A man who is cautious about revealing himself to a woman shows his lack of trust in her.

By deliberately shrouding himself in an enigmatic mystique, Matthew is able to choose the image that he wishes to project; in doing so, he maintains power over the women in his life. To Kate, the sense of mystery fuels excitement about the relationship, conveying the notion that Matthew is a man of many levels. Mary, however, resents the way in which he sets up a barrier that impedes their closeness.

Remember that it is impossible to develop an intimate relationship with an intensely private person unless he loosens up. Drawing him out will become tiresome, as will his accusations that you are invading his private space. Even Kate is likely to grow more irritated and less intrigued by Matthew's mysterious facade.

PUBLIC VERSUS PRIVATE PERSONA

The face that we show to our professional associates and casual acquaintances may sometimes differ from the face that we show our close friends and lovers. However, if the image a man projects publicly is so radically different from the man you know privately that you have to make a major adjustment when you change environments, you may feel that you are leading a schizophrenic existence.

BRIAN: THE LION THAT'S REALLY A PUSSYCAT

Rachel: *Brian is so sweet when we're alone together at home – he is really a liberated man. We divide all the household tasks equally, and he always makes it very clear how much he values our relationship. But when we are out of the house he is entirely different. He becomes very aggressive and macho, insisting on conducting all the communications with waiters and taxi drivers, for example. And he joins in when other men put down their wives and talk about how difficult women are.*

This man may be a sweetheart but he doesn't want the world to know it. On one level, he has accepted the premises of liberation and makes a genuine effort to do his fair share. On another level, however, he maintains some old-fashioned, macho ideas about how a 'real man' should behave. Brian clearly has some conflicts about an egalitarian relationship; by dominating Rachel in public and complaining to others about her, he is trying to lay to rest any notion that he is wimpy or henpecked.

Approach with caution. These vestiges of his upbringing will not be easily dispatched. You can try, however, by making him aware of what he is doing and how it makes you feel. When you are together in a group, go a little overboard to give him centre stage. Let him hear you boasting to others about how strong and successful he is. Although his egalitarian approach to household chores is admirable, find other attributes besides his dishwashing and housekeeping abilities to praise in public.

GREG: DR JEKYLL AND MR HYDE

Sylvia: *My life with Greg would be wonderful if we spent all our time together with other people. In public he is kind, generous, thoughtful and affectionate. More than one friend of mine has told me that I am the luckiest woman in the world. But it is all some sort of perverse act. As soon as we walk through the door of the house, an instant transformation takes place. He becomes critical, nasty, angry and selfish, and I can do nothing right.*

Greg's public image represents only one side of his multifaceted and generally confused personality. Why is his private persona so different? There are several possibilities, each with complex psychological roots. Being close to a woman intimidates some men because they fear the loss of their own identity in a relationship. Some men resent their own dependencies and needs and in a perverse way turn their resentment against the woman to whom they are close. Other men have unrealistic expectations of a relationship and blame the woman for cheating them of their fantasy.

Whether the disparity between his public and private persona has roots in this man's family history or in his emotional past, it will not be easy to dissipate his private anger. He is definitely a candidate for therapy – but will almost surely react with hostility when you suggest it. Without change, you will never be happy with this man.

Early in your relationship, try to arrange social activities that give you the opportunity to watch your man's behaviour in a crowd and how he relates to you in public. Certain facets of a man's personality come to life only in this environment, and it is best to get a glimpse of them before you get too deeply involved.

10

The family tree

The family is the source of madness and the inspiration for genius. It is at the root of a man's capacity to love, the reason for his ability to feel joy, and the source of his deepest insecurity. Those things that make him angry and the accomplishments that make him proud are grounded in his upbringing. From a psychological vantage point, it is almost impossible to underestimate the impact of a man's family.

If you want to know what a man is like, take a look at his father. If you want to know how he relates to women, ask him how he feels about his mother. What sort of a parent will he be? Watch closely when he is interacting with his siblings!

LIFESTYLES

GEOFFREY: ALL FOR ONE AND ONE FOR ALL

Moira: *One of the things that attracted me to Geoffrey was his wonderful family. Being with his parents was just like being with friends. We'd all go out to dinner together – sometimes the four of us and sometimes his brother or sister and their friends, and we had a great time. We even took weekend trips and holidays together. I felt secure and loved by his parents in a way that I had never felt with my own family.*

Geoffrey's primary family unit is the centre of his social and emotional life, and any woman who becomes involved with him must be willing to become a part of it. Close-knit families invariably celebrate holidays together, plan big barbecues and picnics that all are expected to attend, and keep close tabs on everyone's whereabouts. A healthy family is not overbearing, however, but encourages individuality and makes plenty of room for new members.

Families that exclude outsiders, by contrast, tend to crush a man's ego and self-confidence. If he won't stick up for you or tends to ignore you when he is with his family, better think hard about where this relationship can go. But if he is mature enough to juggle family demands with his commitment to you, then you should give him the benefit of the doubt. Just don't try to force him to make a choice.

STUART: DISTANT RELATIONS

Amanda: *Stuart and I have the ideal relationship with our parents. They live in Wales and we live in London. We really enjoy our holiday visits – usually at Christmas and Easter – but after a few days in the confines of my parents' small town, I begin to feel strangled. The geographical distance between us gives us the freedom to live our own lives without interference from our parents. Stuart and I depend on each other and on a handful of close friends for our emotional support.*

Some children deliberately seek to separate themselves by moving far from the family home. Others may be separated from their families merely by circumstance and maintain involvement as best they can by regular visits, telephone calls and correspondence.

Similarly, a 'distant family' is not necessarily one that is far away. Children may live within a few miles of their families and even see them regularly, yet never leap the barrier that impedes emotional closeness. Men who were nurtured too little or protected too much had little positive experience with love in their formative childhood years. The result is difficulty developing emotionally binding relationships as an adult. Whether he continues to live in close proximity to his parents or moves far away, such men are constantly on guard against the possibility that you will seek to control them and will often reject your attempts at intimacy. They often crave close connections, however, and with your patience can learn to open themselves up.

151

DAN: FAMILY SHAME

Tina: *Dan had postponed introducing me to his family for so long that I was convinced he was ashamed of me. It turned out, though, that he felt he really had to apologize for his parents. Visiting his family revealed a side of Dan that I had never seen before. Life in his home was like a scene out of Coronation Street. Although I more fully understood why he sees his family so rarely, I don't think he has acknowledged how much he loses by neglecting his roots. His parents are really loving people; they just have a certain style that can be very grating.*

Tina has correctly observed how important it is that Dan comes to terms with his parents and learns to appreciate their worth. A man who is ashamed of his family carries a secret shame of himself because, like it or not, he is part of them. His harsh judgements on his parents are too easily warped into harsh judgements of himself and those close to him.

One element of maturity is the ability to make peace with your family. Dan must acknowledge his well of anger and accept his parents for better or worse before he will be able to create a happy family of his own.

DEREK: FAMILY COURT

Laura: *Derek prepared me for his family long before we were ever introduced. 'It will be like a trial before a jury' he said, and that turned out to be no exaggeration. I was grilled with questions and examined as though I were under a microscope. What did I do? What did my parents do? What was my relationship with Derek? How long had we known each other? How did we meet?*

Derek was very supportive, which helped, but they certainly made it clear that I wasn't good enough for their son. What really irked me, though, was how they treated Derek. He wasn't good enough for them, either!

A judgmental family minimises each of its members, ensuring that children grow up feeling unworthy and lacking in self-respect. Approach a relationship with such a man judiciously.

By preparing Laura for meeting his parents, Derek proved that he had overcome the liabilities of his past and learned to accept their hostilities and dismiss their criticisms as irrelevant. He introduced her with pride and did what he could to shield her against their barbs, questions and criticisms.

Unfortunately, many men aren't so mature. Instead, they are at once victim and persecutor; having been scrutinised so critically while growing up, they have never learned the virtues of forgiveness, acceptance or patience. As a result, they apply their parents' standards to anyone they meet, especially women with whom they become involved.

CHARLIE: IT'S TRADITION

Beth: Charlie and I fit in so well with each other's families that our match feels as though it is meant to be. Our families are both very traditional and very conservative. Our fathers take charge of things outside the home and our mothers run the household. Maybe I'm old-fashioned, but I think that's great. My parents have led a good life together and I'm looking forward to the same.

After a decade in which they felt increasingly pressured to compete in the job market, some women are now rediscovering the option of being a mother and a homemaker. This does not mean that all achievements of the past decade need vanish. In any relationship based on mutual respect, no woman needs to be in an inferior or submissive role, even if she chooses to work in the home. What *is* important, however, is that expectations be clarified early in any relationship – and be regularly reassessed as lifestyles change.

Beth was genuinely pleased at the role models of her past and perfectly willing to strive towards them. Other women, however, will express dismay to discover they have fallen into the same groove as their parents. And although many relationships begin with pledges of egalitarianism, old and familiar patterns often emerge. A man who grew up in a home in which his mother was chief cook and bottlewasher for his father, may unconsciously expect you to treat him in the same way. Clear channels of communication early in the relationship are critical to prevent this from becoming a problem.

OLIVER: BORN FREE

Barbara: I never could figure out who did what in Oliver's family. His parents were really free spirits and they encouraged their children to be highly independent. Everyone was very

*creative but there wasn't much of a work ethic in the family.
When money ran short, his father or mother would reluctantly
get a steady job, then stick with it only until the bills were paid.
I could see how this led to Oliver's happy-go-lucky attitude to
life and his own creative pursuits, but it just didn't fit in with
my lifestyle. I need a lot more structure and security than he does.*

A nontraditional family can spawn a free spirit – or a man
who rebels by developing a rigid approach to life. The
woman who becomes involved with an independent man
inclined towards bohemianism must be prepared to
sacrifice stability, predictability and security for flexibility,
freedom and a communal life among kindred spirits.
Barbara concluded that the payoff was not worth the risks;
another woman, however, might welcome the opportunity
to leave straitjacketed conventions to dabble in unknown
realms.

THE DIVORCED HOME – FOR BETTER OR WORSE

Because around a third of all marriages now end in divorce,
many men of marriageable age are the progeny of divorced
parents. What are the effects of growing up in a divorced
home?

- As with all traumatic situations in a child's life, a man
  can be strengthened by adversity and determined not to
  repeat his past. Or, he can feel defeated by the past and
  pessimistic about finding marital bliss.
- Studies show that boys in single-parent homes grow up
  faster and assume adult responsibilities earlier. He may
  grow up to be rather serious and conservative, having
  foregone childish behaviour at a young age, but he will
  not run from responsibility.

- Boys raised by single mothers are often particularly close to them and able to communicate openly and discuss their feelings together. In a relationship, this translates into someone who understands the importance of intimate and emotional communication.
- Some men have a sense of emotional deprivation that makes them need a woman's intimacy, If a man blames his mother for his deprivation, however, he may carry the seeds of unresolved anger with him and frame situations in which a woman continually disappoints him.
- Children often blame themselves for their parents' divorce, which can create problems with self-esteem. In later relationships, this man will always apologise or take the blame for mishaps and you will find it difficult to convince him that he is worthy of your love.
- In a bitter divorce each parent may berate the other to their children. You must be very cautious about entering a relationship with a man who was exposed to this on a constant basis; he is inevitably filled with anger, usually towards both parents, and finds it difficult to trust anyone.
- Children who escape the most traumatic effects of divorce can emerge with a heightened awareness about the possibility of good relationships. When a divorce was amicable and both parties remain friendly, they can provide an atmosphere of love and security for their children that enables a man to accept the inevitability of change and approach love sensitively and sensibly.

HIS PARENTS

To understand a man's family Love Codes, the astute woman will look carefully at his maternal and paternal influences and notice how he interacts with his parents. A man is most likely to struggle with internal conflicts if the values of his parents clashed radically. When parents are compatible – or openly acknowledge differences between them and deal with them diplomatically – he is likely to be more confident about himself, although more set in his ways.

A man's relationships with his siblings can also be revealing because they set the pattern for future intimate relationships.

His mother: the first woman in his life

The single most important question you can ask a man you meet is, 'How do you feel about your mother?' Regardless of who you really are, a man will view you through the lens in which he sees his mother, and ultimately he will treat you the way he treats her.

If his answer is negative and you can still detect anger in his voice, approach this relationship with trepidation. A man's mother is the prototype for all his feelings about women, and if he is not comfortable with them, he is not emotionally capable of sustaining a mature relationship with another woman. A man who hates his mother unconsciously hates all women. Even if he also loves and needs a woman in his life, he will play out his anger about his past in your relationship and subject you to deep emotional pain.

Just as a man with negative feelings towards his mother will be critical and suspicious, a man with positive feelings accepts and appreciates the special qualities of a woman. If the bonds between a man and his mother are too tight, however, there may be no space in his life for a new emotional connection.

Observe not only what he says about his mother but how he relates to her. The old adage says that a man who is good to his mother will be good to his wife. Be on the lookout for answers to these questions:

Does he offer her emotional support?

This is a man who can show love and compassion in response to a woman's needs without feeling obliged to agree with her at all times.

Does he share news of his successes and failures with his mother right away?

A man who shares important news with his mother does so because he knows that she will be responsive and supportive to anything he says. A man who is accustomed to positive acceptance knows how to give of himself to other women.

Is he proud to introduce you to his mother?

This is an indication of his respect both for her and for you and illustrates his ability to appreciate a woman's worth.

How often does he speak to or visit his mother?

A man who enjoys his mother's company on a regular basis usually respects the value of a woman's companionship and has egalitarian feelings towards all women.

When he describes how his mother raised him, is he understanding about components of his upbringing that he did not like?

Perfect parents, like perfect spouses, just don't exist. If a man accepts this about his mother, he will also be able to accept it about his wife. Such compassion indicates an ability to discuss problems openly and seek resolutions together.

Does his personality remain the same when he is visiting his parents' home?

A man who has truly cut the apron strings and is comfortable about his own identity is neither intimidated nor rebellious with his parents. He will not bring unresolved conflicts or fears of intimacy into his adult relationships.

His father: A man's first role model

Most middle-class men in their late twenties and older grew up in traditional families in which the mother was the primary care-taker and the most important determinant of a man's feelings towards women. Nonetheless, a man's father serves as an important role model for the way in which a man will relate to a woman. Therefore, the second most important question to ask a man: 'How did your father treat your mother?'

Unless a man consciously rejects his father's approach to

dealing with women, he is likely to repeat the same pattern. Thus, you will want to watch closely to see whether your man's father treats his wife with respect, compassion, sarcasm or cruelty. Is she a confidante and a soul mate? How are responsibilities divided in the household? How does he view his wife's work? Has their relationship changed over the years?

ROOTS GO DEEP – PARENTAL MARRIAGES

How does the combination of different parental personalities affect a man's behaviour in a relationship?

Emotionally Aloof

A man who grows up in a home where both parents are cold and distant about expressing affection assumes this is the normal way of interacting. He is likely to focus more on objects and achievements than on people, because he does not readily make close connections.

Overprotective Mother, Absent Father

Lacking a strong role model, this man never gains sufficient confidence to assert his independence. He has learned, instead, that it is easier to allow women to take care of him.

Depressed Mother

When a mother is too depressed to extend herself for her children, they are certain to suffer emotional deprivation. The result is a man who denies himself pleasure, does not acknowledge his own needs, and can't shake off his own sense of desperation.

A Nurturing Couple

The child of nurturing parents understands the importance of taking care of others. When a man is raised in a loving home, he usually learns to be confident and to develop skills that put others at their ease. Genuinely fond of other people, he is cooperative and trustworthy.

Indulgent Parents

Parents who are excessively indulgent of their children do them no real favours in the long run. Lacking encouragement to mature, a man's emotional development tends to be somewhat stunted.

Critical Mother, Passive Father

Because he has been made to feel humble and inferior to women, the son of a critical mother usually suffers from lack of self-esteem. The problem is intensified by his father's inability to counteract her influence, which may leave him angry and depressed.

Demanding Mother, Underachieving Father

The offspring of such a couple feels compelled to achieve great things but lacks the confidence to do so. Pushed towards goals beyond his capacity or interest, yet lacking a role model to show him the path towards success, he faces contradictory pressures that often become impossible to handle.

SIBLING RIVALRY?

How does he relate to his siblings? And what does it mean for an intimate relationship?

- 'Vincent became the head of the family at the age of 13 when his father died and he assumed serious adult responsibilities.'

A man who assumes a lot of responsibility at an early age – perhaps by caring for an elderly parent or by taking charge of the family finances – will behave responsibly in a relationship. However, he is rather serious about life and often finds it difficult to set aside his role as an authority figure.

- 'Chris hasn't talked to his brother in 15 years.'

A man who is completely out of touch with his siblings demonstrates hostility and an unwillingness to forgive. In a relationship some of that buried anger is sure to surface.

- 'Tim and his brother are best friends, live a few streets from each other, and are in business together.'

Men whose siblings are their best friends know how to maintain the strong emotional connections that you will appreciate in a lover.

- 'Eric visits his family only once a year. If he calls any other time, we know it is to ask for something.'

A brother who calls his siblings only when he needs something from them does not understand that meaningful bonds are a two-way process. He'll expect a lot from you, too, but won't give much of himself.

- 'Rick is privy to all the family gossip but he never expresses an opinion or takes sides.'

A man who remains neutral in all family squabbles, listening without comment to all sides of a dispute, tends to be emotionally detached. You may find it difficult to engage him in dialogue on subjects that he finds threatening, but his ability to see both sides of an issue qualifies him to mediate acceptable compromises.

IT'S ALL IN THE UPBRINGING

Many experts say that half a child's learning takes place before the age of four. In addition to shaping his sense of security and his ability to form close bonds in those early years, a man's family influences his capacity for professional accomplishments later in life. The two case histories that follow illustrate how.

STEVE: BORN TO WIN

Jane: *From the time we were teenagers, it was clear that Steve was destined for success. He was the oldest child and both his parents doted on him and pushed him to achieve. By the time he was 9 years old, he had created his own paper round; when he was 11 he hired his brothers to work for him so that he could branch out into bigger businesses, like delivering groceries and mowing lawns.*

I always admired Steve and as we got older, he began to pursue me with the ardour and determination I had seen him pour into his work. He showered me with phone calls and gifts until I finally relented and we began to go out together. He was the type of man who knew how to get whatever he wanted; he just wouldn't take no for an answer.

Steve learned early in life that persistence is the key to success. From his youngest years he worked hard and constantly set new goals for himself. And he brought those same attributes into his adult relationships with women. Having known Steve from childhood, Jane was a step ahead of women who knew nothing of a man's past. In particular, she knew that his parents' encouragement had given him a positive self-image, one of the important components of a mature emotional relationship.

Full speed ahead here. Steve has the determination, clarity of focus and persistence that will carry a man far. Once he decided that Jane was the woman he wanted, he pursued her with the same vengeance that he pursued career success. Obviously Jane has no way of knowing whether Steve will continue to maintain interest once he wins her over. Nor does she know just how deeply involved she'll want to get with this man. But his persistence makes him a likely candidate for success, and it is certainly worth dating this man to see where it leads.

TOM: THE SEEDS OF DOUBT

Victoria: *Tom has a serious self-image problem. He's actually an accomplished musician and a good carpenter, but he can't shake himself free from his sense of failure. He does tend to leave projects unfinished sometimes, but I'm proud of him and very happy with our life together. I just wish he felt better about himself. The real problem is that he can't match the achievements of his older brother. Well, who can? John is an exceptional man – a superachiever and a nice chap besides! I think his parents played favourites with their sons when they were growing up together.*

Unless parents strive to acknowledge the accomplishments of *all* their children, younger children may have difficulty competing with older siblings. The seeds of failure are planted in early childhood and often have little to do with actual performance. The anticipation of failure, like the expectation of success, can become a self-fulfilling prophecy. As an adult, a self-defined failure may give up instead of pursuing new opportunities. He may make faulty judgements, or take easy paths rather than challenging ones.

Move cautiously before becoming involved with such a man. You will have to spend a great deal of time bolstering his sagging spirits and conveying an optimistic outlook. It is also important to be strong and independent enough to separate your ego from his. Be appreciative if he has been more sensitive and receptive to others because of his disappointments. Be suspect if he is embittered and blames others for his failures.

A man who feels good about his family life will seek to recreate it. The man who feels dissatisfied with his early experiences has a much more complex psychological challenge before him. Ideally, he will identify the gaps in his own upbringing and attempt to include what was lacking. Some men, though, are victims of their own fate, and unconsciously recreate early, unhappy experiences.

11

Emotional scenes

Women choose their men for a range of rational and not-so-rational reasons. Some make their selections purely on the basis of chemistry; others seek a man whose goals and values closely match their own. Whatever the motivation, his emotional profile is the personality factor that probably has the greatest effect on every aspect of your relationship.

Knowing what he will be like to live with at least gives you a fighting chance of deciding whether you really want to. Emotional stability, levels of tension and anxiety (and how he handles it), mood swings and neurotic habits must all be assessed when considering the potential of a relationship. Keep in mind that it is as important to know thyself as to know your mate. Two moody people may be incompatible, for example, but a rock-steady man may be just the ticket for a woman whose emotions travel a roller-coaster path.

Although some men may be adept at masking their emotions, unconscious Emotional Love Codes cannot be readily hidden from an astute observer. In the next section, we'll run down a list of questions and answers to help you better understand what your man is all about.

WHAT MAKES HIM TICK?

Self-Acceptance

When others point out a fault, can he laugh and acknowledge the criticism? Or does he become upset and withdrawn?

Self-acceptance means acknowledging both one's attributes and failings. A man comfortable with himself is more accepting of others. Someone who is critical of himself also looks for faults in others.

Argument for Argument's Sake

Does he start an argument just for the sake of the intellectual challenge?

Men who like to argue are usually energetic people who thrive on excitement. They may also be angry and manipulative, taking pleasure in asserting their intellectual superiority. There are only two ways to cope with a combative man: either fight back or become his victim.

A Full Schedule

Does he like to work hard and play hard or is he tentative about living life to the fullest?

A full and active life indicates a man who is self-confident, well-organised, goal-oriented and energetic. Don't try to hold him down, because he'll resent you for it, but do take the opportunities that his rich life offers.

A man who is fearful confines his activities to familiar arenas. If you need more action, don't waste your energy trying to push this man forward.

Bend, Don't Break

Is he easily persuaded, rigid in his viewpoints, or willing to evaluate each situation individually?

Flexibility is the key to success in all relationships, but a man who discusses issues as they arise is infinitely more interesting than one who always accedes to your wishes without discussion.

At Ease

Is he comfortable with strangers or constantly worried that things will sour in a new situation?

The man who trusts others and approaches new experiences optimistically adds depth to a meaningful relationship. Once he makes a commitment to you, he is open and perceptive enough to steer it in a positive direction.

Decisions, Decisions

Does he have difficulty making decisions, such as choosing clothes, restaurants, holiday destinations?

A man who can't make up his mind lacks confidence in his own judgements and needs others to counsel him. But if you like to take charge, he might be just the ticket for you.

Don't Take It Personally

When engaged in discussions, does he become embroiled in emotional attacks?

A man of intense emotions can be an amorous sexual partner but his inability to engage in a heated discussion without getting personal shows his lack of maturity. Don't despair, however. If he loves you enough, and you have the patience and fortitude to teach him to control his anger, he has the potential to change.

Giving Thanks

Does he praise and thank you when you do even the smallest favour for him?

A man who is generous in offering praise and saying thanks is one who is generous in spirit and soul. He appreciates a woman and understands that love must be nurtured if it is to last.

Seeking a Scapegoat

Does he complain that others take advantage of him or are out to ruin him?

By blaming others, this man reveals how sorry he feels for himself – but he does not take the responsibility to change his lot in life. Keep away – eventually he is certain to blame you for his misfortunes.

HIS STATE OF MIND

Before probing the Love Codes revealed by certain personality traits, it is important to develop an overall sense of a man's emotional state. In the following quiz, you will select some of his most common moods.

Pick the six words that are most applicable to his usual emotional state:

1. Thrilled
2. Peaceful
3. Indifferent
4. Jittery
5. Agitated

6. Dejected
7. Exuberant
8. Patient
9. Self-absorbed
10. Stressed
11. Furious
12. Downcast
13. Buoyant
14. Tranquil
15. Blasé
16. Apprehensive
17. Hateful
18. Lethargic
19. Blissful
20. Satisfied
21. Submissive
22. Nervous
23. Resentful
24. Glum
25. Cheerful
26. Composed
27. Resigned
28. Anxious
29. Tense
30. Disheartened

List your six choices here:

The Score

Score as follows for each response:

> **5 points:** Traits 1,7,13,19,25.
> **4 points:** Traits 2,8,14,20,26.
> **3 points:** Traits 3,9,15,21,27.
> **2 points:** Traits 4,10,16,22,28.
> **1 point:** Traits 5,11,17,23,29.
> **0 points:** Traits 6,12,18,24,30.

[26 – 30 points]

This man has found the secret of a happy, fulfilling life and approaches each new day with renewed energy and enthusiasm. In a relationship you will find him eternally optimistic and supportive, and if his state of rapture is genuine – and if you can tolerate his endless good cheer – by all means consider getting involved. He'll brook no negativity from you, however, and if his optimism grates on your nerves, better make another choice rather than risk becoming resentful of him.

[21 – 25 points]

In general this man is quite satisfied with his life. Pleasant and levelheaded, he is not one to suffer pangs of self-doubt, depression or unreasonable anxiety. Although he has a rather sentimental side, he is capable of communicating with you in an adult and rational way. Affectionate and kind, he rarely loses his temper, although he can when the provocation is great enough. In general, an ideal candidate for a relationship.

[16 – 20 points]

Although he is well-adjusted, this man feels that his accomplishments have fallen somewhat short of his goals. He expects a relationship to help him turn his life around by providing the stimulation and opportunities that he has been lacking. If you can shake him out of his complacency and tolerate the limits to his passionate side, you will find that he has the capacity to love with conviction.

[11 – 15 points]

This man focuses almost exclusively on his own troubles and has a knack for getting involved in the wrong things. Sometimes he is merely jumpy, other times he is almost frantic, and you may find his angry outbursts and moody introspection hard to take. No need to write him off entirely, however; if you can gain his trust and ease his fears, there may be a chance for a rewarding relationship.

[6 – 10 points]
Here is a hostile man who feels frustrated and powerless about many aspects of his life. Unfortunately, there is no way of gauging the remark or incident that is likely to send him on a tirade so you will often feel that you are walking on eggs when you are together. It doesn't take much to upset him – probably because he is so upset with himself. His rage sometimes emerges in the form of sarcastic remarks and constant putdowns of others, and the best way to deal with him is to steer clear.

[0 – 5 points]
It won't take long to realise how emotionally withdrawn this man really is. Humourless and despondent, he is indifferent to any sort of meaningful communication and won't respond to your efforts to lift him out of his depressed state. In time his grief may pass, but for the moment, he is too difficult to become involved with.

EMOTIONAL PERSONALITY TYPES

The extent of his insecurity, his preference for independent or close involvement, his readiness to become angry and his willingness to express feelings are all basic emotional states that have a significant impact on the course of a relationship. In the following pages we analyse some common emotional states and what they reveal about a man.

Insecurity Versus Security

Insecurity is a state of fear and doubt about one's ability to cope. Everyone feels insecure at some times and in particular arenas, such as at work or in relationships, and a little reassurance goes a long way. In the lives of some men, however, insecurity is so pervasive that it makes intimacy almost impossible.

In emotional interactions, men express their insecurities in many different ways – by being extremely loving and attentive, by being critical and aloof or by acting passively and compliantly. But the roots of the insecurity usually extend back to similar childhoods: lacking approval for early accomplishments, they grow up feeling unworthy and inadequate.

Life with a secure man runs more smoothly and predictably. Because he is so self-confident, he usually demands less of your time and attention. But he may be less willing to make the same intense emotional commitment that a man with stronger needs will.

PATRICK: SOCIAL INSECURITY

Sonia: *Patrick is so insecure I don't dare look at another man when we are together. Even when we're at a party, I know I'll have a big fight on my hands when we get home if I talk to a strange man. That's why I try to maintain an independent social life and prefer going to parties alone.*

Men like Patrick are highly sensitive to perceived slights and are constantly in need of reassurance. A woman with a strong independent streak may not respond well to his demands. On the other hand, a woman who tends to be insecure herself often prefers the safety of a man in whom she has complete faith.

If you become involved with an insecure man, be prepared to commit a lot of energy to soothing his ruffled feathers and establishing a bond of trust between you. Take heart though: once that bond is established, this relationship has the potential to be deeply intimate and honest.

The Issue of Independence

A dependent man is one who leans on a woman for emotional support. Although his vulnerability sometimes seems excessive, a dependent personality is willing to make a commitment to a woman who treats him tenderly. Once he feels assured of your love, he has a lot to offer emotionally and if you thrive on close connections, this could be the man for you.

An independent man, by contrast, will not lean on you but he also cannot be easily cajoled into keeping you company. He may be reluctant to spend a lot of time with your friends and family and won't attend cultural events or other activities with you unless he really enjoys them.

GEORGE: A CONSTANT COMPANION

Maxine: *In the beginning I thought it was so romantic that George wanted us to do everything together. After all, how many men will go shopping with a woman? Or consult her on almost every decision? But after a while I began to feel suffocated. He wouldn't go anywhere without me — except work, of course, and even then he telephoned me constantly. Whenever I made my own plans, his resentment was palpable. I kept urging him to see his friends but apart from of his weekly poker game, he wouldn't budge without me!*

Independent women will find George's inability to function alone rather excessive; they prefer men who also value their own space. Other women crave a coupling as close as this one and will thrive in so much well-meant attention and affection.

Controlling

The impulse to control others has its roots in habit, a resistance to being controlled, and a man's slightly arrogant assumption that he knows what is best for the people he loves.

DON: LIKE A BIRD IN A GILDED CAGE

Ellen: *I always liked a big, powerful man. When we began going out together, Don made all the decisions for both of us and I felt well taken care of. Since we have been seeing each other for a while, though, I have started to feel more like his prisoner. He makes all our social arrangements and insists on dropping me off and picking me up at work. He even tells me what clothes to wear and tries to give instructions to my hairdresser.*

When I protest, he speaks genuinely about the depths of his love and says that he wants the best of everything for me. The dynamics of our relationship are driving me crazy, yet I think it would be hard to find another man who would make me feel so safe and protected.

When they began going out, Ellen was pleased to have Don assume the responsibility for her well-being, but inevitably began to feel stifled in a relationship that more closely resembles that of a parent and child than of two adult lovers. Although a woman who grew up without the certainty of parental love may be willing to sacrifice a degree of autonomy for security, Don's demands are extreme.

By denying Ellen the right to her personal space, Don essentially tries to control her life. Unless she is willing to surrender her sense of self to Don, Ellen will eventually have to gather the courage to set limits on his control. When she does, the depth of his commitment to her will be visible in his willingness to yield to her needs.

Angry

Some men habitually respond with anger to almost any conversation. This stems from a reservoir of anger and frustration that has accumulated over the years, especially during childhood. It is important that they vent their anger productively by channelling it into appropriate occupational and recreational pursuits.

JERRY: NOT THE LAST ANGRY MAN

Lydia: *The first time I met Jerry, he was reprimanding a man for smoking in the lift. I was impressed with his courage and concern, but I've since learned that he is always ready to argue. He picks fights with me, quarrels with friends and complains about trivial slights from waiters.*

Lydia did not find it easy to remove herself from Jerry's anger, but she was ultimately confronted by the need to detach herself from his irrational emotional responses or leave him altogether. Two types of women will survive in a relationship with a man who angers as readily as Jerry: someone who has a calm disposition, a strong ego and is relatively free from anger herself, or a woman who needs to vent her own anger and thrives on the challenge of a heated debate.

Signs of a Simmering Volcano

Totally avoid the man whose anger manifests itself in physical violence, persistent emotional abuse or antisocial behaviour. There are no sterling qualities sufficient to compensate for the loss of your emotional or physical well-being. An irrationally violent response to provocation or the suggestion that he has been involved in illegal activities or is a heavy drug user, are clear warnings to stay away.

Trust your instincts if you sense that something is amiss, because the clues that tip you off are not always obvious. Even casual remarks can indicate a deeper disturbance, especially if there is a pattern among them.

Here are some clues to emotional abuse:

- Hanging up the telephone in anger.
- Not returning phone calls.
- Berating you in public.
- Criticising the way you dress or talk.
- Blaming you for mishaps.
- Making hurtful remarks to you or others, especially by deliberately mentioning sensitive topics.
- A sadistic sense of humour or practical jokes that are harmful or embarrassing.
- Cruelty in word or deed, especially to those who are vulnerable, such as animals, children or the elderly.
- Striking or hitting you.

Here is evidence of antisocial behaviour:

- Lying about where he spent an evening or who he was with.
- Bragging about escapades that never happened.
- Falsifying his family history, his professional credentials or his accomplishments in order to impress you.
- Abusing people, such as waiters, shop assistants and employees.
- Not tipping or failing to reward a person adequately for services rendered.
- Trying to get away with something – such as not repaying a loan, shoplifting or not returning borrowed items.
- Turning an argument into a physical confrontation.
- Anger about perceived slights, such as having to wait to be served or being jostled.

Compulsive

Conditioned to believe that spontaneity leads to error and impulsive action creates danger, a compulsive man's outlook on life tends to be somewhat rigid. Although he is usually aware of this trait, such a man cannot function effectively unless he is doing things his own way. Don't expect him to change significantly despite prodding from you.

JONATHAN: NEAT AS A PIN

Gail: *Who says that a man can't be as neat as a woman? Disorder is Jonathan's nemesis. He is a little extreme but after all the sloppy men I have known, I am grateful to be involved with someone who cares about order and appearance. Although some of his habits drove me crazy at first, such as lining up his shoes and removing my clothes from behind the door, I am willing to accept his fastidiousness because he offers me so much in the other realms of our relationship.*

Although Gail did not share Jonathan's excessive sense of order, she was willing to compromise for the other rewards in their relationship. In particular, she was aware that compulsive men are usually stable and secure, and that certain compulsive habits, such as financial planning, and household organisation contribute to success in our society.

But some women find a man like Jonathan, who needs to plan his life down to the last details, too rigid for their tastes. His approach is particularly anathema to a freewheeling and spontaneous woman.

Non Emotional

The non emotional man keeps his feelings under a tight lid, a trait that appeals to some women and drives others mad. As long as he can deal comfortably with your mood swings, the decision is yours as to whether your emotional makeup is compatible with his. The man to avoid is one who considers your displays of emotion unseemly and childish. He will be critical and undermine even your wish to talk about feelings.

MALCOLM: THE STOIC SUPPORTER

Nicki: *In any given hour my emotions can roller coaster from tears to euphoria to anger. But Malcolm is a real stoic, the voice of reason in the midst of my hysteria. No matter how I react, he responds in a calm, cool and collected manner that eventually relaxes me. My friends find him a bit cold, but that's just what I need − ice water on my hot head.*

Although he is not particularly emotional himself, Malcolm accepts a woman's need to vent *her* emotions. He thus provided Nicki with the sounding board that allowed her to explode without risk. Curiously, his non emotional personality may also appeal to a woman inclined to suppress her own emotions.

Many women, however, will feel deprived by Malcolm's detached approach to his emotional reality, because the ability to share feelings is one of the basics of intimacy. Do not get involved with this man if you cannot function happily with someone who represses strong emotion. The trade-off between open communication and a safe but superficial relationship will quickly become unacceptable to you.

THE SYMPTOMS TO WATCH OUT FOR

To master the art of selecting the right lover, you must be able to extract larger meanings from small behavioural clues. The anecdotes that follow paint portraits of men who are exhibiting the classic signs of certain emotional types. At their best, these traits can be positive and productive. When they become excessive, however, they are magnified to a point at which they are out of control and self-destructive.

If you are to choose your man wisely, you'll need to understand the Love Codes behind his actions and be able to distinguish healthy from unhealthy behaviour.

Is He Dissatisfied or Depressed?

Everyone feels a bit dissatisfied from time to time, but a depressed man carries that feeling to extremes. Someone who is merely dissatisfied accepts the need to make changes in his life and responds to the support and suggestions of others. A chronically depressed man, by contrast, lives as if a black cloud hangs constantly over his life.

Here is how you can recognise a true depressive:

- He is never satisfied with himself or anyone around him.
- He always anticipates the worst and finds little joy in life.

181

- He has unrealistically high expectations that are doomed to be dashed.
- He blames others for his failures.

Although a compassionate woman can lend her support to a man who suffers from infrequent bouts of depression, relatively few women can be happy with someone who is chronically depressed, because the emotion is so contagious. Women who repeatedly become involved with depressed men are often depressed and angry themselves.

Is He Cautious or Anxious?

Caution and concern can be appropriate and useful responses to certain situations. Feeling tense about a new undertaking may prompt us to analyse it more carefully; for example, nervousness about a job interview may motivate us to prepare for it. Inappropriate or all-consuming anxiety, however, is usually a symptom of deep-seated insecurity and mistrust.

Because an anxious man does not feel confident that he can cope with events as they occur, he is uncomfortable with spontaneity and very resistant to change.

Here is how you can recognise a man who is afraid of his own shadow:

- He anticipates catastrophic outcomes from minor events.
- He is preoccupied with what others think of him.
- He looks back at an event and fears that he said or did the wrong thing.

A woman who becomes involved with him must be alert because anxiety can be chronic and all-pervasive. By focusing on the minute worries of daily life, he may deny deeper emotions. It will be difficult to get past his anxiety and his need for constant reassurance, and there may be few moments when you share good feelings together.

Is He Perceptive or Paranoid?

A perceptive man is one who can read the messages being relayed by subtle signals. Someone who combines natural astuteness with a generosity of spirit that encourages others to seek his advice is a rare and special friend indeed.

Unfortunately, hyper-awareness in tandem with self-doubts can become warped and self-destructive. The perceptive man known for his willingness to help his friends can become the paranoiac who believes others are secretly plotting against him. Ironically, this assumption often stems from his own feelings of anger towards others.

Here is how you can identify a man whose judgment has been clouded by anxiety:

- He interprets completely innocuous statements as highly personal and negative judgments.
- He feels that the laughter and glances of others are directed towards him.
- He mistrusts the generosity of others, seeing it as an attempt to manipulate him.

No matter how perceptive he is about others, the paranoid man will have moments when he doesn't trust anyone – even you.

Is He an Eternal Optimist?

A man who has a positive outlook and expresses confidence in his ability to cope with the world can be a joyful companion. His eye is always fixed on the brighter side of life and such enthusiasm can be contagious.

But the eternal optimist operates on the basis of denial, ignoring all negative feelings in order to shield themselves from the intense sadness that underlies a happy-go-lucky demeanour.

Here's how you can recognise the man who carries good cheer to extremes:

- He never acknowledges negative feelings – yours, his, or those of anyone else.
- He is always prepared to find an excuse for other people, even when their behaviour is clearly inappropriate.
- He refuses to anticipate problems – hence, he has no plans for a rainy day.
- He acknowledges neither the past nor the future but lives only in today's sunny present.

A man who blocks out deep emotions is uncomfortable in a close love relationship, because it is the willingness to share private feelings that provides the foundation for intimacy. Admittedly, many successful relationships are formed on the basis of common activities, with minimal emotional interaction. However, a woman who seeks psychological intimacy with her partner will feel unfulfilled with a man who cannot relate on that level.

Is He Health-Conscious or a Hypochondriac?

A man's concern about his health and well-being is admirable and indicates that he is also concerned about maintaining healthy relationships. When he focuses on every ache and pain in his body, however, it is an indication that he is using these concerns to express other feelings.

Watch for these signals of a real hypochondriac:

- He either cannot acknowledge, or doesn't realise, his true feelings, both physically and emotionally.
- He is preoccupied with his bodily functions and expresses his anxiety through them.

- He complains about imaginary ailments and exaggerates minor symptoms in order to attract attention and sympathy.
- His self-indulgence emerges only in his complaints of illness. In all other ways he appears to function as a responsible and caring adult.

A patient woman who correctly perceives his complaints as symptoms of anxiety and the need for attention can learn to love this man. Because there is a childlike quality to his emotional state, a hypochondriac is often receptive to the observations of others and will acknowledge his psychological condition, even if he doesn't change it.

Is He Energetic or Frenetic?

Whether they are driven by ambition, a passion for activity or a commitment to a wide range of time-consuming interests, some men simply cannot keep still. There is a clear distinction between the merely energetic man, who is productive but emotionally mature, and the frenetic man, who keeps busy every single moment of the day in order to avoid facing his inner fears.

Here is what the man who is perpetually on the run does:

- He dissipates tension and controls strong emotions by focusing outwards.
- He never does only one thing at a time.
- He overschedules himself and spreads himself thin.
- He never says no to a new idea or a new friend.
- He never gives all of himself to one project or to one person.

Although it can be stimulating to share your life with an active, even hyperactive man, he may have a tendency to ignore the woman he is involved with in his rush to fulfil other commitments. A man who operates at a level of high energy creates a mood of tension around him, and the woman he is with must be able to shield herself from his stress.

Is He a Charmer or a Manipulator?

The charmer frequently delights in pleasing others and thinks of himself as someone who brings joy into the lives of others. Foot-loose and fancy-free, he can be a delightful companion because he is not burdened by the responsibilities most conventional people assume in the course of their lives. However, he may also be an expert at manipulating others into taking care of him.

Here's how you can recognise the manipulative man:

- He feels that he is entitled to whatever he can get from other people.
- He's very generous when he's flush, but usually he is 'waiting for a cheque' or has 'left his wallet at home'.
- He is always boasting about some pie-in-the-sky deal but doesn't have any concrete plans for the future.
- He doesn't repay loans.

An otherwise serious and responsible woman may be attracted to a charmer because he enables her to act out her fantasies of rebellion. But be careful about over-investing in this man – either emotionally or financially.

Is He Self-Indulgent or an Addict?

A man who knows how to relax and enjoy himself is a delightful and affectionate companion. A good bottle of wine and a hearty dinner, a few pounds won or lost on a football game, or several hours spent on the golf course are reasonable indulgences that provide a release from stress and tension.

It is when the indulgence becomes his central preoccupation – to the point of interfering with his personal life – that self-destructive addiction has developed.

Here are some of the traits of a man who travels over the border separating self-indulgence from addiction:

- He repeatedly and habitually engages in self-destructive acts.
- He uses addiction as an excuse to avoid strong emotions.
- He dreads emotional and personal confrontations.
- He is emotionally immature and dependent.
- He consistently opts for instant gratification rather than working towards longer-term goals.

Severe addictions can wreak havoc on the lives of anyone who becomes emotionally involved with them. Many different types of women have a pattern of repeated involvement with addicts – some see themselves as long-suffering martyrs, others are driven by the desire to dominate a weaker man. Whatever her personality type, the woman who repeatedly becomes involved with addictive personalities does so to avoid confronting emotional pressure.

Most emotional types are neither positive nor negative, although some types of men admittedly are more difficult to live with than others. The woman who thrives with a difficult man is someone who relishes challenge and risk and fears boredom. Not for her is the easygoing, stable relationship that can be deeply satisfying to a woman who thrives on consistency and predictability.

The better a woman understands her own personality type, the more likely she is to make a wise choice among the men who interest her. What makes you happy and secure? What kind of a pay-off are you willing to strike between independence and security ? How do you react to a man who is not emotionally responsive? What balance between passivity and aggression is most suitable to your needs?

If you are honest with yourself as you consider these questions, your chances of striking the right match may increase dramatically.

12

The price of success

In our society, money is not only our medium of exchange but a measure of status, achievement and capability. As a result, both men and women tend to confuse success with earning capacity.

Actually, though, success is a subjective judgment, which is inextricably linked to an individual's personal priorities. Mother Teresa and Rupert Murdoch are both successful – in very different ways, of course. Some women define a successful man as one who has attained the trappings of power and brings home a hefty salary, regardless of his emotional makeup. Others shrug off financial achievement in favour of personal autonomy or the pursuit of artistic endeavours. Regardless of her definition, every woman seeks a man whose success she can respect.

A successful man has a healthy outlook on life, generally appreciates his good fortune and takes setbacks – financial and otherwise – in his stride. As a result, he is accepting, rather than critical, of other people, and is ready to offer his help when he can. In a relationship, he will be generous not only with his credit card but with his time and emotional energy as well.

The man to avoid is the one whose greatest ambition in life is keeping his wallet full. Centuries ago a wise man asked: 'What has a man profited, if he shall gain the whole world, and lose his own soul?' Unfortunately, many women choose men who don't know the answer to that question.

In this chapter we look at the pay-offs that are sometimes made between financial and relationship success and assess the Love Codes hidden in a man's approach to money.

His Glass Is Always Half Empty

No matter how they are praised, admired and rewarded, some men never feel satisfied with their own achievements.

Although such dissatisfaction can be a powerful driving force, it also indicates someone who is obsessed with his own performance. Beware the man who looks at others and feels that he can never match their accomplishments. As a lover, he will be convinced that you've been with better, sexier men in the past, and that he's not worthy of you.

Conversely, if he decides that he *is* worthy of your affections, then he'll conclude you're not good enough for him and lose interest. If he really interests you, try to make him aware of what he's doing, but don't expect miracles – he will have to confront his basic sense of inadequacy head-on if he is to change.

Through Rose-Coloured Glasses

Equally unrealistic is the man guilty of the sin of pride, an arrogant braggart convinced that his accomplishments are unrivalled. Ultimately, he is sure to get his come-uppance, in part because he lacks the self-awareness to assess realistically his own strengths and weaknesses. In the meantime, steer clear. His false sense of superiority will come through loud and clear in an emotional relationship, where he will never admit to being wrong. He'll expect you to trust his judgment and let him have his own way.

SUCCESSFUL PREDICTIONS

Success and failure are more a matter of nurture than nature, but from childhood some people seem bred for success, whereas others appear destined for failure. Think back to your school days and you will surely remember a range of personality types. Remember the aggressive kid who became the natural leader on the playground? And the teacher's pets, the shrinking violets, and the butts of other children's cruelty? How about those who stuck tenaciously to the task of solving a puzzle and others who gave up as soon as they became frustrated?

Obviously certain predictors of success are inherited. Good looks, high intelligence and athletic ability are natural endowments that can be cultivated but not created from scratch. Still other traits – such as aggressiveness, determination and patience – are a mixture of natural aptitude and learned ability. By looking closely at your man's personality traits and natural abilities, a woman can make a fairly accurate guess as to his likelihood of success – both personally and professionally.

SIGNS OF SUCCESS

Regardless of their fields of endeavour, successful people usually have a number of traits in common. Among them:

- A sense of purpose.
- An ability to define achievable goals.
- Internal motivation and commitment to an end product.
- A willingness to take risks and bounce back from disappointment.
- A willingness to work hard.
- Patience to face and overcome obstacles.
- Tenaciousness and determination.
- The strength to seek advice and learn from others while ultimately keeping one's own counsel.
- Self-confidence.
- A sense of self-worth.

SIGNS OF FAILURE

There are also common threads running through the personalities of those who regularly fail at what they undertake. Such men seldom have the capacity to maintain a mature relationship because they are intimidated by the responsibility involved.

Watch your man for signs of these handicaps:

- Failure to define his goals and the steps necessary to achieve them.
- The tendency to live in a fantasy world rather than to think realistically about his strengths and shortcomings.
- A low frustration tolerance that tends to make him give up easily or leave tasks unfinished.
- Laziness or distractibility.
- Lack of discipline or misplaced discipline (i.e. he tends to work hard in purposeless activities).
- Fear of success, perhaps because he feels that he does not deserve it.
- Fear of change, fear of competition, fear of failure.
- Arrogance or denial.
- Efforts to impress others by name dropping or the boasting of past successes.
- Concealed or apparent nervousness.
- Sour grapes or negative attitudes or excuses.
- Jealousy, envy, or put-down of others.
- A poor self-image or the lack of self-worth.

WHAT IS HIS POTENTIAL FOR SUCCESS?

Answer each question with Yes, Sometimes, or No:

1. When he is wrongly criticised, does he stand his ground and defend his actions?

2. Does he have the ability to remain calm and collected in the face of opposition?
3. Before making a major decision, does he carefully weigh all its pros and cons?
4. Is he able to explain a task to others so that they can do the job he expects?
5. Does he maintain cordial friendships with business acquaintances?
6. Does he initiate projects without being asked?
7. Once he makes up his mind, having weighed up all the facts, is it difficult to dissuade him from his decision?
8. Does he search carefully to find the person best qualified to do a job?
9. Will he defend a friend or employee who is being treated unfairly by others?
10. Is he appropriately cautious about investing money with casual acquaintances or those unknown to him?
11. When he is asked to do a time-consuming and tedious job, will he stick to it until it is completed?
12. When he fails, is he quick to pick himself up and try again?

The Score

5 points for every Yes; 3 points for Sometimes; 1 point for No.

[50 – 60 points]
Success is a function of perseverance, initiative and loyalty, and this man ranks high in each one of these areas. Obviously self-confident and single-minded, he's got the characteristics of a high achiever and is likely to get what he wants from life.

This man is used to following his impulses and reaping the rewards. Nagging will get you nowhere with this man; he has a strong streak of independence and won't be receptive to your efforts to change him. However, he will put the same effort into pursuing you as he does into pursuing success – if he decides you're the woman he wants.

[40 – 49 points]
Although this man also has a great capacity for success, he is just a touch less aggressive than the highest scorer and may not have the consuming determination necessary for outstanding achievement.

Conversely, there is more room for emotional involvement in his life. If your suggestions are carefully timed and tactfully phrased, he will listen gratefully and respond. Use your influence on him carefully, however – he tends to be a little cocky and if he perceives your efforts as an attempt to gain control of the relationship, he is likely to turn cool.

[30 – 39 points]
This man's top priority is not professional success. He has some initiative and determination but doesn't possess much of the follow-through required for exceptional achievement. Don't expect him to rise to stratospheric heights. With a little encouragement, however, he will settle into a stable job in the middle ranks of his career and be moderately successful.

An emotionally satisfying relationship is quite possible with this man. He is not overly caught up in his work, yet has some of the attributes desirable in an intimate relationship. Check his answers on questions 3,4,5,8,9,10 and 12. If the answers are 'yes', full speed ahead for the woman who does not overrate the value of professional accomplishments.

[19 – 29 points]
It is doubtful that this man will ever achieve major successes. Despite his good intentions, he lacks the strength of purpose to make his visions a reality. Timid about his

convictions, he will probably opt to settle into a steady, salaried position that doesn't demand much energy from him. Reconsider if your dreams are ambitious ones. But if you are as laid-back and easygoing as he is, and share his limited goals, then proceed forward.

[Below 19 points]
Proceed with caution, because this is a very poor prospect. He is programmed to fail at almost anything he tries. Unless you relish the idea of constantly picking him up and brushing him off – only to see him fall right back down again – it's probably best to seek a more suitable candidate.

BALANCING EMOTIONAL AND FINANCIAL SUCCESS

Lucky is the woman who finds a man whose success has not been obtained at high emotional cost. Although sound finances and emotional maturity are far from incompatible, some men don't seem able to put energy into obtaining both.

Alas, when one is sacrificed at the expense of the other, there are usually negative personal and professional consequences. Sometimes the single-minded pursuit of money enables a man to hide from his emotions. Other times his efforts to attain emotional maturity seem to cripple his commitment to work.

Financial Successes – Emotional Failures

The 1980s seem to have spawned a generation of professional workaholics for whom career success is an overwhelmingly important source of satisfaction. But men who focus single-mindedly on career achievements are often uncomfortable in emotionally charged interpersonal relationships. Rather than admit to being vulnerable, they concentrate their energies on the external manifestations of success. The self-image problems of a man who confuses net worth with self-worth usually result in vapid love relationships.

Here are the problems you can expect with the man who is a financial success but an emotional failure:

- He may be a good provider but he'll tolerate few emotional demands.
- He will not be available to share family responsibilities and problems.
- Although he is committed to your relationship, he will insist on maintaining an uncomfortably high degree of independence.

Some of the most sought-after men are workaholics. Why do women pursue them with such interest? Partly because they are at the pinnacle of their success and convey enthusiasm not only about their work, but about life itself. And partly because their personal and financial power is a very appealing attribute.

Only a woman who has strong and independent interests of her own is likely to find a workaholic a very desirable candidate for love. The following portraits paint two different types of workaholics.

TIM: ALL WORK AND NO PLAY

Andrea: *Tim and I went out for three years before I discovered how limited our relationship was. I know that sounds crazy, but we had always stressed the importance of maintaining independent lives. Between building my own career, socialising and trying to stay fit, I was really very busy and quite satisfied. Only when he started pressuring me to get married did I realise how far apart we had grown.*

The reason was obvious. Tim worked all the time. He ran his own business and never found time to take a holiday or even a long weekend away. At night he was too tired for sex, and in the morning he was too tired to talk (and vice versa). I think he wanted to get married simply because it was convenient; certainly not because he was willing to put renewed energy into our stale relationship.

Extreme caution here. A workaholic like Tim is essentially a one-dimensional man who pours all of his passion into work and retains none of it for life's other pleasures. His interest in marriage did not derive from genuine devotion to Andrea but from a sense that marriage was the appropriate and proper course for a man in his position.

The fault in this situation does not lie exclusively with Tim however. For three years Andrea allowed their relationship to drag on and never stepped back from her own busy life to acknowledge its limitations and to try to change the situation. A healthy relationship requires that both parties keep their eye on its development and communicate with each other when problems begin to arise. Yet not all communication is what it appears to be.

SAM: BULLISH ON BUSINESS

Bridget: *Sam called me at work several times a day to talk endlessly about his business dealings. At first this made me feel very important in his life, but eventually I realised how limited the range of his interests was. He never asked about me and we never tackled emotional issues unless I raised them. In fact, business and money were the only subjects that Sam really cared about.*

In the beginning of a relationship, it is easy to mistake conversation about business for meaningful communication. This is a time when you are filled with curiosity about his life. Perhaps you feel flattered when he takes you into his confidence and see it as a reflection of his interest in you. But Bridget initially failed to see that Sam's conversation did not represent true *communication*. In its ideal form, a shared dialogue means an exchange of interests and feelings; at least some of the time, those feelings should be personal and focused on the two of you.

Balancing Emotional and Financial Success

Fortunately, there is cause for hope. All financially success-ful men are *not* emotional adolescents. And some who are are willing to change.

One method is to shower a man with love and attention. Although most of his passion may be poured into bank statements and stock investments, an open man can be very susceptible to an adoring woman willing to help him cultivate his emotional side. This is particularly true of an older man. Having already established himself professionally and attained a degree of financial independence, he may at last be ready for the challenge of an intimate relationship.

Emotional Success — Financial Failure

Some men are financial failures because:

- They are intimidated by the need to compete with other men.
- They fear the risk of failure.
- They unconsciously believe themselves unworthy of it.
- They place their artistic visions or personal preferences above the drive to make money.

Many men who refuse to conform to society's traditional expectations cultivate their emotional needs to the exclusion of their professional ones. A woman's ability to be happy with such a man depends mostly on her personal priorities and financial needs.

ANDY: CAN THERE BE CAKE WHEN THERE IS NO BREAD?

Maggie: *Andy is the sweetest, most loving and generous man I've ever met, but he has absolutely no interest in making money or improving his lifestyle. I respect his determination to succeed as an actor, but in his mid-thirties I think he needs to be more realistic about the odds and seek a different path. He's highly disciplined about his acting classes and rehearsals, and thoroughly lazy about seeking better-paid work. When funds get tight, he'll take the first odd job that comes along, but he'll quit in a minute if an acting opportunity comes up, even if it pays absolutely nothing.*

There is an element of selfishness and a hint of adolescent behaviour in a man too stubborn to change for the good of a relationship. A man who scoffs at the importance of material possessions often has an unrealistic attitude towards life and relies on others to take care of him.

The key to a relationship with a man unable to earn a decent income is his lover's ability to adjust to the situation. A woman who is willing to live on a limited income or assume breadwinning responsibilities in return for emotional closeness and personal power, could find this relationship eminently satisfying. After all, how many of us crave a man who is happy, faithful, emotionally involved and supportive?

But this is not the right man for a woman who needs to be financially secure or is interested in the high achiever willing to play by the rules for success.

Making Sense of his Money

Money is frequently cited as the primary source of marital discord. Because of its importance in our society, it has a value that far transcends its worth as a medium of exchange, becoming instead the means by which we express ourselves and communicate with others. It reflects our feelings of self-worth, love and power.

The way a man builds his personal assets often matches the evolution of emotions. Some men spend cautiously and place most of their assets in secure, steady investments, such as Gilt Edged Securities. Others live for the moment, and when they do invest, gamble on stocks and shares, hoping for greater gains.

INVESTING IN YOUR RELATIONSHIP

The ways in which a man invests his money tell you the kinds of risks he's willing to take in life and how much effort he will put into a relationship.

1. Gilt Edged Securities

This man does not like to take risks and prefers the security of limited goals. If he likes you, he will be willing to commit to a relationship readily and remain satisfied and loyal.

2. Day-to-Day Savings and Money Market

Like his assets, this man likes to keep his relationships fluid. He wants to have control over any eventualities that may arise and often continues to seek other women while dating one, just in case a better opportunity comes along.

3. Stocks and Shares

Here's a gambler who trusts his instincts and thrives on the excitement of new possibilities. He's the kind of man who'll jump into a relationship, but is open to trading if he thinks the growth potential is limited here.

Understanding the Love Codes behind a man's financial approach will give you a deeper understanding of his prospects as a lifetime partner.

GERALD: AUDITING A RELATIONSHIP

Fran: *Although Gerald was earning tons of money, and investing it wisely, he still kept a record of every penny he spent. He resented the cost of entertaining, never took holidays and*

*resisted buying new clothes. He made me account for every penny
I spent. And he was stingy in other ways, too – our
lovemaking was bland, devoid of any real intensity or intimacy.*

Gerald is a poignant example of why money can't buy
happiness. Although he acquires money to feel secure, the
fear of losing it actually intensifies his insecurity. His
tension and rigid behaviour make him incapable of
meaningful love.

Is THIS MAN A GOOD LOVE RISK?

1. **If he needs to purchase a particular item does he
   wait for it to go on sale?**

   a. Usually.
   b. No.
   c. Yes.

2. **Does he overspend in order to impress other people?**

   a. No.
   b. Yes.
   c. Occasionally.

3. **If he has a limited clothing budget, does he:**

   a. Buy one expensive suit.
   b. Purchase several inexpensive garments.
   c. Repair and update the apparel he already owns.

4. **What does he do with his old newspapers
   and magazines?**

   a. Saves them in piles all over his home.

b. Throws them out every day.

c. Keeps a few of the ones that contain important articles.

5. **When using toothpaste or paper towels, does he:**

   a. Use more than he actually has to?
   b. Use less than he actually should?
   c. Use about the right amount?

6. **When it comes to items that spoil, such as fruit, vegetables or milk, does he:**

   a. Tend to buy more than he needs?
   b. Tend to buy less than he needs?
   c. Buy just the right amount?

7. **Does he turn off the lights and appliances in his house or flat when they are not being used?**

   a. Always.
   b. Sometimes.
   c. Never.

8. **What does he do at a restaurant when there is too much food to eat?**

   a. Asks for a doggie bag.
   b. Lets the food be cleared away.
   c. Attempts to finish everything on his plate.

9. **When paying for a meal in a restaurant, or buying clothes or other items, will he:**

   a. Always use a credit card?
   b. Sometimes use a credit card?
   c. Rely strictly on cash?

10. If he drives a car, is the vehicle:

    a.   Expensive and beyond his means?
    b.   A little too small and economical for his lifetstyle?
    c.   One that truly reflects his income?

The Score

Add together the points scored for each question to get the total score.

```
1.  a/4   b/2   c/6
2.  a/6   b/2   c/4
3.  a/2   b/4   c/6
4.  a/6   b/2   c/4
5.  a/2   b/6   c/4
6.  a/2   b/6   c/4
7.  a/6   b/4   c/2
8.  a/4   b/2   c/6
9.  a/2   b/4   c/6
10. a/2   b/6   c/4
```

[50 – 60 points]

This man is a cautious, practical individual who is not prone to taking financial risks. He is more likely to put his money into securities and mutual funds than to risk them in speculative stocks. Conservative and responsible, only the security of a solid economic base makes him feel comfortable.

His choice in a partner is similarly based on practical considerations. Don't expect a whirlwind romance or intense passion from him. This man is searching for a woman whose goals and values are compatible with his own; when he finds her, he will treat her kindly and well. He is rigid in his ways, however, and does not take kindly to criticism, so don't expect impractical gifts from him.

[40 – 49 points]

Slightly more carefree, this man takes a few well-informed risks now and then but never goes too far out on a financial limb. Although he may put a small amount of his funds into questionable investments, the bulk of his assets remain secure in low-risk, low-investment accounts.

Surprises aren't welcomed by this man. He can accept, even appreciate, a woman with a bit of charming idiosyncrasy, but he is basically serious about proper behaviour and generally plays by the rules. He is a good prospect if you value responsibility without excessive frills.

[30 – 39 points]

This score suggests a man who is frugal one day then swept away by his desires the next. He can be very conservative and then, suddenly, succumb to an impulsive urge to buy an extravagant possession. In general, he is financially responsible, but he has been known to undo years of good investment through one high-risk adventure. Some men in this category have gambling instincts that can lead them into serious difficulties if they let down their guard.

If you meet this man during one of his impulsive moments, he may sweep you off your feet. But momentary exhilaration can turn into terrifying insecurity if you do not have ample financial and emotional resources of your own. Better be sure that he's willing to allow you to handle the family finances before trusting your fates to him.

[20 – 29 points]

This man is extravagant to the point of wastefulness. He lives for the moment because no one ever schooled him in the necessity of saving for a rainy day. His boisterous and lackadaisical attitude towards money often extends to his relationships. He's rather careless with his affections and a bit insensitive in showing his appreciation of your efforts.

This man's wastefulness and big-spender mentality is a source of irritation to many women, especially when he starts spending their money. If he's got plenty of cash, sit back and enjoy it while it lasts. Watch out, though, if he is living beyond his means. As soon as he reaches his credit card limits, he'll be looking to you when the bill arrives.

From the earliest moments of a relationship, pay close attention to the way he talks about success and money. Do finances consume only a reasonable proportion of his attention? Does he successfully balance the time he devotes to money-making enterprises with the energy he puts into love relationships? Are his fiscal investments sound ones or based on get-rich-quick schemes?

Unless you can answer yes to all three questions, better keep a close watch on this man. If financial success is your motivation for pursuing a relationship, then full speed ahead. But don't expect much emotional interaction. Keep your distance if money is not your main priority.

13

Are you sexually compatible?

There is probably nothing so steeped in legend, lore and fantasy as sex. It is the arena in which contented couples remind each other of the depths of their love and the theatre where the discontent express their frustration and anger. The bedroom is an adult playground where, in the best of times, the deepest intimacy possible between two human beings can be obtained.

A large percentage of the population report sexual problems or dissatisfaction with their sex life. And this despite the sexual revolution of the 1960s, when the virtues of free love were widely touted and inhibitions were supposed to be shed. Who are these people? Did they live through the revolution without ever taking a gun from their holsters? Do they suffer from personal inadequacy? Have they failed to read enough about the techniques of good loving? Probably not.

More likely they are people who accepted many of the newly granted freedoms licensed in the newspapers and on television. In those days, the rule was: If you are attracted to someone, you should naturally have sex. And if you were sexually compatible, the relationship could be considered meaningful. In those days, all powers of decision making were handed over to the genitals. Women were told to do it and to talk about it, to search for their G-spots and to strive for multiple orgasms, to experiment with different partners and different positions, and to love it all!

But, as with so many revolutions, romantic myths have inevitably given way to harsher realities. Good sex has not proved to be a matter of keeping score or of constantly seeking new partners and exotic experiences. Instead, most of us have finally discovered that sex is satisfying only when it is an integral part of an emotionally rich relationship. This chapter is aimed at helping you learn what you need to know to find the man who has also learned that lesson.

A MATTER OF BIOLOGY

Many women confuse the intimacy of sex with emotional intimacy and assume that a physically expressive man is equally open about his feelings. Conversely, many men distinguish sex from emotional involvement, compartmentalising their feelings in a way that totally mystifies women. The tenderness of a man's lovemaking may as easily stem from his own need for closeness as from genuine feelings for a woman.

Like it or not, biology plays a big part in a man's sex drive. A man with a high sex drive may consciously perfect his techniques in order to enhance his sex appeal – and his own ego as well. Curiously, many men who lead lives on the fringe of conventional society are great lovers. Daunted by the tasks of competing in life, they focus their energies on developing powerful sexual connections with women.

A man with a low sex drive, by contrast, may never have given sexual behaviour much priority and therefore feels inexperienced or inadequate in sexual interaction. Otherwise successful and confident professional men often have hang-ups that stem from a fear of sexual intimacy.

A man's sexual nature, of course, is expressed not only in the sexual act itself but in the ease with which he makes casual physical contact, the sensual pleasures he enjoys and the types of women to whom he is attracted. As you analyse a man's sexual proclivities, watch for Love Codes that tell you whether he is aggressive or passive, nurturing or demanding, aloof or intimate, dominant or submissive, faithful or philandering, caring or cruel, stable or unstable, imaginative or boring and involved or indifferent.

FLIRTING – DOES HE MEAN TO STAY?

A man who flirts either verbally or nonverbally is sending you a flattering message and you have the right to be pleased. Whether it is a sign of true affection, sexual attraction or merely a passing compliment depends on what follows next. Even if flirtation doesn't actually lead to sexual involvement, a man's approach reveals a lot about his attitudes and how he will conduct himself in a relationship.

Suggestive Signs

- **The Look in his eye:** The suggestive way in which a man eyes you tells you a lot about his intent. A furtive

glance, for example, suggests that he is interested, but finds you a bit intimidating. A raised eyebrow is a cockier sign, and a direct stare is a deliberate effort to pierce your defences and sweep you off your feet.

- **Smiling through:** Another clue to the intention of his flirtatiousness is the sincerity of his smile. A warm, open smile suggests genuine interest; a tense or closed smile is a sign that the flirt is rather unsure of himself and may distrust women.

- **Whistling:** Although this is not the mark of a sophisticated man, whistling is generally harmless and is not intended as a serious flirtation. Men will usually whistle at a woman only when they are in the company of other men. It is a way of simultaneously acknowledging your appeal and declaring themselves off-limits at the same time.

- **Licking his lips:** Although many women find this explicitly sexual gesture to be obnoxious and degrading, it is an indication of a sexually passionate man. If you are looking for thrills – and don't need much intellectual intercourse – he may be your man.
- **Humour:** A man with a sense of humour is charming and endearing enough to dispel potentially awkward situations with a clever remark. However, he is uncomfortable in the role of aggressor and needs you to give him the confidence to continue his advances.
- **Touching:** A man who touches you when you are first introduced is bold, confident and sensual. He is ruled by his passions and uses that passionate nature as a means of asserting control in a relationship. If you share his sensual side, all signals are go here.
- **Complimenting:** Some men are sincere with their compliments, whereas others use flattery solely for the purpose of getting ahead. Pay attention to what he says – if he goes overboard in praising your beauty or intelligence, it is wise to be somewhat sceptical. But if his remarks are appropriate to the conversation, you may have found a man who is not afraid to say what he really feels.

FOREPLAY: A TASTE OF THINGS TO COME

Most sexual encounters begin with arousing words, games or other techniques to ease a couple from a social evening into a night of lovemaking. What a man likes to do prior to the main event hints not only at his abilities as a lover but at many other aspects of his personality. Along with analysing his preferred methods of foreplay, watch his actions for these clues: does he always initiate foreplay? does he always like to do the same things before lovemaking? does he linger to enjoy foreplay or does he rush through it?

Massage

It is hard to go wrong with a man who likes to massage you. He communicates patience and caring as he strokes and kneads those knots from your body. Here is a man who understands the sources of tension in the modern world and responds to a call for help in times of trouble. High praise for someone who knows that a good massage is a fine way to begin a relaxing evening of lovemaking.

Necking and Petting

A wise and thorough man knows slow and arousing stimulation starts from the top down. Necking is the traditional method of working into sex, and for good reason; it is a way of gradually building intimacy and excitement. The man who enjoys necking and petting has a strong sentimental side to him and is capable of great infatuation.

Sex Films and Photos

Although looking at sex films and photos can be a stimulating and interesting diversion for a couple, men usually find them much more arousing than women. Be careful here – the man who always looks at visual erotica prior to sex is not adequately attracted to his own partner. He is keeping women at a distance in order to avoid feeling vulnerable to them.

Dressing Up

A man who wants to dress in costume before he undresses for lovemaking has a unique and playful imagination. His lack of inhibitions and refreshingly unselfconscious nature translate nicely into creative lovemaking. Be cautious about his intentions, though. If he always insists on dressing up, watch out! This man doesn't really want to be with *you*.

Sharing Fantasies

Fantasies are a good way to warm up to serious sexual activity. Even very close couples are sometimes too inhibited to share their deepest, darkest secrets, and a man who is willing to expose his fantasies to your scrutiny is able to open up in other realms of his life as well. Sharing fantasies is also a fine tool to improve intimate contact.

Getting High on Booze or Pot

Some men use a little alcohol or marijuana to relax before a sexual encounter. In moderation, some drugs can intensify physical sensations and increase pleasure, but in excess they are more likely to make him limp, not aroused. A man too ill at ease to enjoy sober sex probably has other emotional problems that will surface in the course of your relationship.

Bubble Bath

Taking a bubble bath together is a sensual way to begin an evening together. You both emerge relaxed, aroused and reassured that anything can safely go in the bedroom. You can look hopefully at the man who suggests a warm bath before bed.

MEN WHO PLAY THE FIELD

The sexual magnetism that draws lovers together is powerful and mysterious. People are attracted to each other for many reasons, and it is not always possible to understand just why. One thing is certain, however: women are drawn to men who can meet their emotional needs, whatever those may be. Whether it is for a single night or for a lifetime, a woman looks to a man for the comfort, security, passion, commitment or pain she unconsciously craves.

In the following section, we provide sketches of some of the men who inhabit the sexual landscape and explain what their behaviour means to a sexual relationship.

Don Juan

The perennial 'ladies' man' charms, flatters, and seduces any woman he can – and makes her feel wonderful about it. A man said to be a Don Juan actively pursues a coterie of different ladies and is in no hurry to settle down with any of them.

> Kim: *When I first spotted John at a party, my internal warning system told me that he was a flirtatious ladies' man. My rational side warned me to be cautious, but my passionate side took no heed. When John held me close and whispered those tender words of appreciation, I felt myself begin to soar. And when we made love, his caress was so tender I felt as if our souls were merging. By the next morning I was in love and ready to run off together into the sunset. And John was prepared to run off into the sunrise, appreciative of a lovely but final evening together.*

Don Juans are men who live for the moment, and during that moment they are genuinely tender and appreciative. But they are inherently restless, fearing intimacy as much as they need it, often avoiding long-term attachments to mask a deep-seated dependency. At parties, you can recognise them because they are surrounded by attractive women, and they ask for every phone number in the crowd. Well-meaning friends are also certain to point them out as men who have left a string of old lovers behind.

Most Don Juans eventually settle down, but only when the desire to start a family or the feelings of loneliness become overpowering. And even then, sexual fidelity never becomes their strong point. They are constantly battling against a sense of suffocation and may flirt or even have an affair simply to reaffirm their independence.

Playing the Field

A man who plays the field may seem genuinely interested in you, but he disappears from sight after the first time you sleep with him. What's going on here?

> Gina: *If I am really interested in a man, I might want to spend the night with him. But even after things go really well, I have been with men who left the next morning and never called me again. It didn't seem to matter how long it took to have sex – whether I held out till the third date or the tenth date, after sex he disappeared. After all these years I still can't tell when a man is really interested in a relationship or just another sexual conquest.*

Although the notion is an archaic one, there *are* still men who pursue women with the goal of sexual conquest. Try not to take rejection personally. A man who heads for the hills after having sex with a woman assumes she will make demands on his time and emotional energies. Perhaps he has had genuinely bad experiences with clinging women, but more likely he is simply afraid of intimacy.

Here are clues that suggest your man may not hang around for too long:

- He falls madly in love and hotly pursues you without knowing who you really are.
- He tells you everything you've always wanted to hear – that you're wonderful and that he's been looking for someone like you his whole life.
- He is too physically expressive, touching and stroking you before you are on intimate terms.
- He's never been involved in a long relationship.
- Rumour or his own information suggests that a lot of women have passed through his life.
- He is boastful or patently dishonest about his background.
- He shows off by spending a lot of money.
- He plies you with alcohol.
- He is overly eager to have sex *before* you go out together.

Although playing the field usually signals the fear of commitment, there are ways to overcome his mistrust. If you are interested in pursuing a relationship with this man, you will have to convince him that you are perfectly comfortable with casual, obligation-free dating.

Here is how to convey that message:

- Steer clear of talk about commitment and relationships. Even if you are speaking abstractly, this is sure to make him nervous.
- Let him know that you have an active social life. See other men and chat casually about your social and professional pastimes. Don't say yes each time he asks you out.
- Don't always press him to arrange plans for your next rendezvous.
- Play him at his own game by saying that although you like him and enjoy his company, you prefer to play the field for a while.
- Do not have sex on the first date.

If you reassure your man enough to begin seeing him on a regular basis, you will have to determine his desire for a permanent relationship by reading other Love Codes. Is he interested in you and your activities? Is he attentive and caring? Do you share the same goals and values? Does he have close male friends? What is his relationship history? Is he at a stage in life when commitment makes sense?

Once he finally decides to make a commitment, this man can be surprisingly faithful and dependable.

Passive Passion

The passive man is someone afraid to make the first move. He looks for aggressive women who will take charge.

219

Monica: *I knew Evan was really interested in me, but he was awkward and hesitant so I finally made the first pass. I was not surprised when he responded enthusiastically, but then he kept stepping away to ask me what I liked. I didn't want to discourage him, though, so I made some specific suggestions. He was agreeable to everything I wanted and amazingly had no problem performing!*

Evan's ability to respond sexually was predicated on Monica's willingness to reassure and guide him. Although a passive man lacks the self-confidence to initiate sexual activity, he is generally able to open himself up both physically and emotionally once he knows what is expected of him. Evan's timidity will drive some women away, but with patience and a bit of imagination, others will find him a nurturing lover and a devoted partner. He is sensitive to your needs and accepts your ideas in guiding the relationship.

Caution: Do not confuse passivity with passive-aggressiveness. A passive-aggressive man harbours anger beneath his placid exterior and is more likely to lash out at you than to respond to your well-intended suggestions.

Aggressive Amour

Mary: *Andrew was overtly sexual and up-front about his desires, and I was really turned on by the sexual self-confidence he exuded. I wasn't disappointed either. He was a master performer and a thorough, concerned lover. Although I'm not usually so passive, Andrew seemed determined to take control, and I was willing to lie back and just indulge myself.*

An aggressive lover can be very exciting to a woman, because surrendering control plays an important role in many sexual fantasies. Although the stereotype is a very traditional one, many women still seek a man who is powerful enough to sweep her off her feet.

A man who projects blunt sexuality and the promise of passionate lovemaking so unabashedly is very confident about his abilities in bed. The price of such confidence is often detachment, however. Men who are more emotionally involved in their sexuality are not always able to perform as instantaneously and with as much control. The psychic support you get from this man is likely to be minimal.

Slow and Sensual

Paula: *Max and I can kiss for hours before we even get around to stroking each other. Our physical rapport is slow and sensual as though each part of our body is communicating its own messages. Making love with Max is like having a seven-course banquet. I love the variety and the pacing. Every once in a while, though, I would enjoy skipping the gourmet dinner and just having a hot dog on the run.*

A sensual man perceives each part of lovemaking as meaningful and special in its own right. Reaching orgasm is not his driving goal; rather, it is the process of getting there that provides him with the most satisfaction. Even though you may never succeed in getting a sensual man to forego the fullness of each sexual experience, the consolation is that he cares enough about you to take time with you in other ways too – sharing thoughts, listening to your concerns and lending his support when you need it.

An impatient woman – or one who is not completely comfortable with sex – may become frustrated with the tempo, but if you can slow down to his speed, you are likely to discover new ways to appreciate familiar experiences.

CARNAL KNOWLEDGE:
THE POSITION HE PUTS YOU IN

Although the Karma Sutra lists more than 600 sexual positions, many couples quickly find a few favourites and then experiment with others over time. Variety is an important sexual spice, and in a healthy partnership a couple explore new positions not only to prevent staleness but for the thrill of shared adventure. Similarly, there are many ways to stimulate each other to orgasm, and secure lovers are not afraid of experimentation.

From the first time you and your partner make love, you should observe the sexual positions he prefers and the ways in which he attains – and helps you attain – orgasm.

1. Does he usually want to make love in the classic missionary position where he is on top and you are on the bottom?
2. Does he prefer positions in which you face away from him?
3. Does he experiment with new positions?
4. During lovemaking is he constantly changing positions faster than you would like?
5. Does he insist on controlling all sexual manoeuvres?
6. Is he preoccupied with attaining mutual orgasm or does he focus on the orgasm alone rather than the total experience?
7. Can he reach orgasm only through oral sex?
8. Only through masturbation?
9. Does he attempt to delay orgasm (when he can) so that you can reach yours (when you're close)?

If he usually prefers face-to-face intercourse and experiments with a variety of sexual positions and styles of achieving orgasm, this man seeks intimacy and interacts comfortably with his sexual partners. On the contrary, if he prefers not to face his partner, focuses single-mindedly on achieving orgasm or usually masturbates to reach it, and shifts sexual positions frequently, he is avoiding intense emotions and close personal involvement. There is reason to doubt his ability or interest in making emotional commitments.

Responses that indicate rigid patterns – such as the man always being on top, or orgasm being achieved exclusively through oral sex – signal a need for control that undoubtedly extends beyond the boundaries of the bedroom. Proceed with extreme caution. This man neither understands, nor cares much about, practising the art of a shared relationship. He views women primarily as objects to serve him.

POSTCOITAL PLEASURES

The way in which a man treats you after making love is as revealing as foreplay. This is a vulnerable period for you, and his behaviour after sex is a window to his true feelings about you.

Hugs and Holds You

This man feels protective and loving and expresses those emotions not only during lovemaking but at many other times as well. Your emotional support means a great deal to him.

Wants to Talk

The Love Codes in this behaviour depend on the topics he raises. It can be a time for frank conversation, when he speaks endearingly of your importance in his life and when you feel very close. But if talks about things that are totally irrelevant to the two of you, it could be a sign, once again, that he doesn't want you to get too close.

Eats

It can be fun to share a snack together – whether it is cold chicken or ice cream – after the exertion of lovemaking. This is a healthy sign that shows he is relaxed and comfortable with you – unless he really gorges himself. This suggests that he feels dissatisfied and has to fulfil himself in other ways.

Smokes a Cigarette

A leisurely smoke after lovemaking may seem like a fine way to relax, but it also puts some distance between you. As involved and passionate as he is during lovemaking, he also finds the experience anxiety producing and may have some problems with exposing his emotions.

Goes to the Bathroom

If he visits the bathroom only briefly, you can assume this is a normal physiological function. If he disappears for a long period of time, however, it indicates that he is trying to escape emotional responsibilities and probably feels uncomfortable with intense involvements.

Washes a lot

Although cleanliness may be next to godliness, it is not a good sign after evening sex. It usually discloses discomfort with natural body functions and a feeling that sex itself is dirty.

Turns on the Television

If he snaps on the television the instant you have finished making love, he may be avoiding you, and there is reason for concern. If he hugs and kisses you for a while first, then watching television with you at his side is only a tool for further relaxation.

Goes to Sleep

Nothing is more disconcerting to a woman than the man who immediately goes to sleep after climaxing, because it makes her feel that she is being used merely as a sexual object. If this becomes a regular pattern, this man doesn't really want to be intimate with you. He is expressing his anxiety and detachment with a snore.

IS HE REALLY YOUR DREAM COME TRUE?

There are few better ways to gauge a person's true emotional state than the position in which he sleeps after you have made love.

MATTHEW: SPREAD-EAGLED AND DOMINANT

Cathy: Matthew has a spacious king size bed in his flat, but after sleeping with him a few nights I realised that he didn't really like to share it with anyone. He sleeps spread-eagled across the entire bed as though he is the only one there. And he sleeps so deeply that a gentle nudge has no effect whatsoever.

Just as he dominates the bed, so Matthew must dominate every other situation in which he finds himself. Powerful and uncompromising, he insists on making all the decisions for people around him and demands to be the centre of attention. It is not only space that he allocates parsimoniously – he gives grudgingly of his emotions as well. Be prepared for a relationship with a man who shares himself only on his terms.

Other Sleeping Positions

Foetal

Sleeping in the foetal position reflects the desire to return to the safety of the womb. The man who sleeps most securely curled up into a ball seeks a woman who can provide the maternal qualities he yearns for. He wants a woman of strength and resourcefulness who will nurture his talents and provide refuge for him at the end of the day.

Spoon

A man who wraps his body around you while he sleeps is unconsciously helping you feel protected and loved. He thrives on playing the role of provider, has a strong romantic streak to his personality, and will do almost anything to make your life safe and secure. By contrast, if he wants you to spoon around him, he has strong dependency needs and will expect you to be protective and reassuring. If you alternate spooning each other, your relationship is likely to be a mutually satisfying and interdependent one.

Flat-out

Lying on his back with his legs straight out and hands clasped on his stomach, this man is mature, realistic and devoid of illusions about the world. If you aren't looking for a starry-eyed romantic, you will find him generous and sympathetic to your needs. He has the confidence to face a crisis head-on and to fight for his principles. In a relationship he is calm and rational; only the utmost emotional provocation can make him lose his cool.

Belly down

Sleeping on his stomach displays confidence and a sense of security. He can literally turn his back on the world without feeling suspicious or anxious. If you become more deeply involved with him, no doubt this quality of self-assurance will become even more apparent. By sleeping on his stomach, however, he is also protecting his genitals. This indicates that, despite his passion, he likes to call the tune when he's ready to make love.

Fists clenched

This is a combative position and it discloses unresolved anger that has accumulated either during the day or between the two of you. There's something troubling him and you have to be able to find out what it is. Sleeping with his fists under the pillow means he's the type who hides his anger, whereas exposed fists reveal that he's more open about expressing his feelings.

Arms and legs crossed

Legs crossed shows a particular reticence about engaging in sexual relations, because it is one more way of guarding the genitals. Arms crossed is a way of maintaining distance. In a very real sense, he's not allowing his heart to come close to yours. Before he'll let his guard down, a man who sleeps in this position has to be convinced of your genuine concern and affection for him.

On the edge

The man who moves all the way over to the edge of the bed is usually a passive person who is anxious to please and fearful of confrontation. Despite his protestations that he is concerned only about your comfort, he is also avoiding the intimacy of cuddling together, a reticence likely to carry into other components of a close relationship.

Turning his back

By burying his head in the pillow and turning his back to you, your man is detaching himself from all the upsets of the day, and from his personal relationships as well. Although this position demonstrates his confidence that he has everything under control, it also suggests a capacity to hide his true emotions that is often disturbing to the women he is with.

PERFORMANCE ANXIETY: WHAT HE REALLY FEARS

It should come as no surprise that anxiety, the plague of contemporary times, readily intrudes into the bedroom. Not only are we literally naked during sex, but we are also stripped of our usual defences. Verbal manoeuvres and dossiers of achievement serve no purpose. There is no way to cover up our physical shortcomings and little hope of masking our insecurity. In short, we are forced to be ourselves in bed, an intimidating prospect that can heighten a man's sense of vulnerability.

Increased aggressiveness, distancing, rigidity and emotional withdrawal are all expressions of tension – a major factor in inhibiting sexual performance. Because he is so emotional, an anxious man can be very caring and loyal if he is not defeated by his own anxiety. It may be a struggle, however, to dissuade him from looking for excuses for his own discomfort, such as 'I wasn't really turned on.'

Why Can't He Relax?

Here are some of the reasons a man becomes anxious in bed:

- He is self-conscious and uncomfortable about beginning a new relationship.
- Because he is overly eager to please, he focuses more on his performance than on the joy of mutual pleasure.
- He fears women and generally avoids close relationships.
- He has a history of unsatisfactory sexual experiences or suffers from feelings of inadequacy in many realms of his life.
- Physiology often has a role to play in performance anxiety; a man who is not in top physical form may feel uncomfortable or self-conscious about his own body.

How Can I Assuage His Anxiety?

- Don't blame yourself. A man who is anxious is not intentionally rejecting the woman he is with. The problem is often quite the opposite – too much desire, not too little.
- Regardless of the cause of his anxiety, your reassurance and acceptance can work wonders. If he knows that you are not judging him and that you can be sexually satisfied in many ways other than intercourse, a man may be able to overcome his fear as he becomes more comfortable with you. Don't be surprised, however, if he feels so embarrassed by his sexual performance that he simply vanishes from your sight.
- Watch for behavioural signs that suggest he is anxious about sex. These can include physical symptoms such as cold hands, sweaty palms or rapid breathing; a race

through the preliminaries of foreplay, a reluctance to sit close to you, or obvious awkwardness in his mannerisms. If you want to save this budding relationship, try to slow down the progression into the bedroom, regardless of the pressure he exerts.

DOES HE HARBOUR HOMOSEXUAL TENDENCIES?

A startling number of men have had homosexual encounters or fantasies in their life. Although a single experience certainly does not signal a closet homosexual, frequent experiences or fantasies over a long period of time suggest that latent homosexuality may be lodged deep in a man's psyche. Whether or not he ever acts on his feelings, or even becomes consciously aware of them, they can interfere with his ability to love a woman deeply. Latent homosexuality often lies at the root of a man's unwillingness to make a commitment.

Answer 'Yes' or 'No' to each of the following questions and tally the total number of 'Yes' responses:

1. Does he rail against homosexuality to the point of obsession?
2. Has he had several adult homosexual experiences or does he fantasise about them?
3. On social occasions, is he very reserved and formal in expressing affection towards other men?
4. Or is he so affectionate with his male friends that you feel uncomfortable?
5. Has he told you that gay men periodically make passes at him?
6. Does he feel compassion towards his mother who he views as a victim of his father's rage?

7. Is he especially resentful of the way his mother may have seduced, rejected, or tried to control him?
8. Does he like to tease or make jokes at the expense of homosexuals?
9. Are there times when he suggests another man join the two of you for a sexual 'threesome'?
10. Does he continue to seek the approval of other men that he didn't get from his father?

The Score

If your man scores between 7 and 10 points, you have reason to be extremely concerned about his potential for maintaining a lasting heterosexual relationship. Short of a burning desire to deal with his latent tendencies, which may be helped by psychological therapy, there is little you can do to change him.

A score between 4 and 7 suggests that he may have conflicts in a heterosexual partnership. Before you become deeply involved with him, discuss those conflicts candidly and be certain that he has plans for working them out.

A score between 0 and 3 points is appropriate for an average male and does not indicate latent homosexuality.

Our deepest connections are those with men who remind us of our earliest love objects, often our fathers. Ideally, that person met your needs for love and nurturing and you will seek someone else who will do the same. Too often, though, a woman makes her connections with a man who does not come up to scratch, just like the first man she loved. Unless she recognises this pattern, she may blame her lover for her unhappiness and seek to change him rather than making a more appropriate choice.

Analysing the Love Codes in a man's behaviour before becoming deeply involved can help a woman avoid a serious mistake. In particular, scrutinise his actions before, during, and after sexual play, where important clues to his feelings about women are lodged.

14

Will he ever tie the knot?

How can you tell when a man is ready to settle down? Do men really run from commitment? What can his past love affairs tell you about this one? How do you choose a good marriage prospect – and win him over? Those are the questions that haunt the single woman eager for a long-term relationship. Most of us can tell a tale of woe about a man who talked a good line about marriage, but never set a date. On the other hand, we've all heard those legendary stories about a man who led the life of a playboy until he connected with a woman who swept him off his feet and carried him away to the altar. How do you know what to expect from a man?

If you are really serious about making a commitment and settling down, it is important to read his marriage and relationship Love Codes accurately. This chapter will help you distinguish between the man who will never marry and the one who is genuinely waiting for the right woman. The information here also shows how to identify the attributes of a good marriage partner and how to persuade him to commit.

HOW DOES HE BEHAVE IN A RELATIONSHIP?

In order to know as early as possible whether a man is ready for a long-term relationship, you've got to read any Love Codes you can find – in casual social settings, early dates and private conversations – to take his measure.

Here's a quiz to help you prune down your list of possible candidates:

1. On a date, he prefers to take you to:

    a.   A romantic, first-rate restaurant.

    b.   A trendy night club.

    c.   A private place where you can have a quiet conversation and relax.

    d.   A terrific party where he knows lots of people.

2. Does he:

    a.   Tell you exactly what to do?

    b.   View you as his equal?

    c.   Cherish you while maintaining his self-respect?

    d.   Indulge your every whim?

3. He finds you most attractive when you're wearing:

    a.   An expensive designer outfit.

    b.   A tight dress or trousers.

    c.   A conservative outfit that doesn't draw attention.

    d.   Clothes that you have designed yourself.

4. When you go out, he likes to wear:

    a.   An impeccable designer suit.

    b.   A nice casual jacket with smart trousers.

    c.   Prewashed jeans with a denim shirt.

    d.   A different outfit each time.

5. Does he often:

    a.   Put you on a pedestal by flattering you?

    b.   Act cheerfully and seem pleased to be with you?

    c.   Behave totally in love one day and distant the next?

    d.   Pay attention to you although remaining polite and reserved?

6. If you create a scene at a party, he will be:

    a.   Mortified.

    b.   Angry.

c. Ready to come to your defence.
d. Totally oblivious.

7. **If you flirt with another man at a party, he reacts by:**

   a. Coming on to another woman.
   b. Competing with the interloper for your attention.
   c. Acting slighted.
   d. Looking on in amusement.

8. **In a delicate social situation, does he:**

   a. Adhere to conventions only when they make sense to him?
   b. Disregard the rules because he feels they don't apply to him?
   c. Conform to the norms when he can without feeling unduly concerned about them?
   d. Rigidly adhere to all the rules?

9. **When he takes you out, does he:**

   a. Ask you to make all the arrangements?
   b. Allow the evening to unfold spontaneously?
   c. Consult you as he makes plans?
   d. Create an evening's itinerary without considering your preferences?

10. **When the two of you first met, he:**

    a. Asked a lot of questions and listened attentively to your response.
    b. Tried to impress you with how successful he was.
    c. Talked only about subjects that interested him.
    d. Engaged you in lively and genuine dialogue.

The Score

Match your answers to the following list, then add up your points.

1. a/6   b/4   c/2   d/8
2. a/8   b/4   c/6   d/2
3. a/8   b/6   c/2   d/4
4. a/8   b/2   c/4   d/6
5. a/8   b/6   c/4   d/2
6. a/8   b/6   c/2   d/4
7. a/8   b/2   c/4   d/6
8. a/6   b/8   c/4   d/2
9. a/2   b/4   c/6   d/8
10. a/2   b/8   c/4   d/6

[66 – 80 points]
This is a forthright and ambitious kind of man. Plucky, tenacious and determined, his first concern is making a good impression on others. His strength and outgoing personality sometimes cause him to be a bit insensitive and self-centred in a relationship, but he is generous with his many possessions and lots of fun to be with. If there is even a hint of insecurity beneath his confident exterior, he'll never let you see it.

Style tends to be more important to him than substance, and he is attracted to glamorous and successful women. Feel flattered by his interest – he would not have been drawn to you if you had not made a stunning impression. He loves to be admired and if you can measure up to his standards, your life together can be exciting – high living in high style.

[51 – 65 points]
This score indicates a self-confident, self-motivated and rather sophisticated gentleman. He has good manners and does everything with a certain flair. Style is important to

him but so is substance, and this is reflected in his sophisticated and witty humour. Although he is used to taking charge, he is very considerate and is willing to yield to your needs, as long as they are reasonable. This man is looking for a woman who is his equal but not his competitor. He expects her to be a lady who shares his penchant for romance and sensuality.

[36 – 50 points]

Here is a man who has at least one foot in the 1960s. He has an egalitarian, laissez-faire attitude not only towards relationships but towards life itself. He is uncomfortable in confrontational situations and resists any effort to make rigid plans. Although he is compassionate, loving and gentle, he is also temperamental and prone to wide emotional swings – one moment he's elated and the next moment he's feeling blue.

He attributes his moods to his creative spirit and expects a lot of empathetic support from you. Despite his positive traits, he's got a streak of narcissism in his personality that makes him demand a lot of attention. Although he wants you to understand the depths of his emotions, he is often reluctant to expose himself too much.

[20 – 35 points]

Stability is the attribute that shines through in this man. There's nothing flashy about him; on the contrary, he is cautious and conservative. He's reserved with those he doesn't know well – some say he is a bit stand offish. Don't mistake cautiousness for insecurity, though. He is a man who knows what he wants in life and, in his own quiet way, he can be quite assertive about pursuing his objectives.

His sensibilities are conventional and a wife and family are an important part of his personal vision. Proceed if you think you are his type – he will work hard to please a woman who appreciates his loyal and protective instincts, and his friends find him sympathetic and generous.

HOW CAN I TELL WHETHER HE'LL MAKE A GOOD HUSBAND?

Although personal preferences certainly play a large part in determining a successful relationship, some attributes are an important component of any successful relationship. And, conversely, some men demonstrate so many negative traits that a relationship is almost surely doomed.

A Likely Candidate

Think he really is a good marriage prospect? You could well be right if:

- His parents are happily married.
- He has a healthy and positive relationship with his mother.

- His siblings and many other family members are married.
- He talks openly about his desire for children and a stable home life.
- He accepts responsibility and likes his job.
- He comes from an ethnic or religious background where marriage and family are important.
- He was previously married or has lived with a woman within the past seven years.
- He is not interested in the singles scene.
- His close friends are married.
- He enjoys time alone with you.
- He tells others about you.

Qualities of a Good Husband

No man will have every one or even most of the qualities listed below. Select the 10 attributes you value most from among those listed, plus any others that are of special importance to you. Then give the go ahead only to men who demonstrate 7 of your top 10 qualities. Better examine your motives closely if you are involved with a man who does not meet these standards.

Flexible	Considerate	Kind
Communicative	Trusting	Confident
Attractive	Courageous	Sensitive
Helpful	Honest	Sympathetic
Tolerant	Genuine	Warm
Caring	Loyal	Committed
Consistent	Appreciative	Sense of humour
Financially secure	Friendly	Affectionate
Family oriented	Independent	Sexually satisfying
Intellectual		

Bad News

Have you doubts about this man's desirability as a marriage partner? Don't waste too much time hoping he'll change – you may pass up a lot of other opportunities if you do. Proceed with caution if:

- He is angry at women.
- He has a history of unhappy relationships.
- He thinks marriage is a terrible institution.
- He tells you he's a bad relationship risk (even if he also says that he wants to settle down).
- He's still in love with his ex-wife, childhood sweetheart, or anyone else.
- He feels he's not ready for a relationship.
- He's a poor sleeper or has other finicky habits that make it more comfortable for him to live alone.
- He has many single male friends and enjoys partying and group activities.
- His career is the most important thing in his life.
- He's very individualistic and requires a lot of privacy.

Qualities of a Loser

Although everyone has faults, a man who possesses five or more of the following undesirable qualities has some serious shortcomings. Think carefully before concluding that you will be able to live with this man. If you are seriously involved with a man who has the traits of a loser, it may be time to look honestly at your own motives: are you using the problems of your lover to hide your own problems?

Rigid	Closed	Unattractive
Intolerant	Stubborn	Indifferent
Irresponsible	Sexually unappealing	Cowardly

Inconsiderate	Naive	Dishonest
Phony	Hostile	Dependent
Mean	Insensitive	Cold
Dull	Disloyal	Humourless
Angry	Addicted	Jealous
Irritable	A loner	Critical
Moody	Judgmental	Unfaithful

Elements of a Successful Relationship

The surest predictor of a good marriage is a good relationship. If you can honestly say that your current affair features most of the following characteristics, the odds of a healthy and satisfying marriage soar:

- Mutual respect and acceptance
- Congruent goals and values
- Emotional compatibility
- Constructive openness and honesty
- Physical attraction and harmonious sexuality
- Shared interests and activities
- Expressions of affection and appreciation
- Realistic expectations

FALSE ALARMS: RELATIONSHIPS THAT LOOK GOOD BUT AREN'T

Sometimes a man seems like an ideal marriage candidate but turns out to be terrified of long-term relationships. Other men initiate relationships that seem to be heading towards commitment but turn out to be false alarms. How can you recognise a dead-end involvement?

PHIL: INSTANT INFATUATION

Maggie: *Phil really fooled me. I told myself he was too good to be true, but he really won me over. Phone calls, flowers and dinner every night. Weekends away. Passionate sex. Planned trips away. I really began to believe this could be the true love I'd been longing for. It lasted three glorious months, and then one weekend he was suddenly moody and very distant. I confronted him but he denied that anything was wrong. And he never called me again.*

Some men fall in and out of love quickly, each time genuinely believing that they have found the woman of their dreams. Men like Phil are in love with the *idea* of love, but they find the reality very difficult to sustain.

Unfortunately, it can be difficult to distinguish between transitory infatuation and genuine 'love at first sight', which sometimes blossoms into a permanent relationship. Two clues: how often in the past has he thought himself madly in love? How intense is his immediate pursuit? The more frequently and intensely he goes through the same experience, the more likely he is a victim of 'instant infatuation'.

GRAHAM: THE JUGGLER

Rita: *Graham was very up-front about wanting to see other women. We dated for three years and grew increasingly close, but he continued to insist on an open relationship. He had been married once, he said, and vowed never again to become stifled in an exclusive relationship.*

Some divorced men are very eager to plunge right back into a committed relationship, whereas others thirst for the freedom lost during their married years. If he wants to play the field for a while, it may be because he is fearful of failing again in an intimate relationship – or he may just feel more

243

satisfied indulging himself in the company of many different women. Don't wait too long before asking point-blank if he ultimately desires a relationship with just one woman.

MIKE: ALWAYS INVOLVED, NEVER COMMITTED

Stephanie: *In the course of eight years Mike lived with five different women, each for a year or two. We started seeing each other shortly after he had broken up with the last one and, within a few weeks, he invited me to live with him. I knew from his past history that he was not asking for a permanent commitment – he just hated being alone. And I knew, too, that like his other relationships, ours would end if I gave him a marriage ultimatum.*

Mike appreciates women, and while he is involved he is a considerate and loyal lover. A serially monogamous man, however, either has an overpowering fear of permanent commitment or a problem dealing with deep emotions. Because he tends to have a mellow disposition, it is easy to mistake him for a great catch; that means it is important to learn more about this man's past history and look for other revealing Love Codes. In general, it is wise to be wary of the motives of any man who wants to live together too quickly.

TONY: THE STRINGER

Christine: *Tony has been stringing me along for two years now. Every time I threaten to leave if we don't get married, he begs for a little more time. First, it was to pay off his bills, then it was to save more money; now he needs to get settled in his new job. The next excuse is sure to be that we should wait until we can afford a better home. I did move out once and he coaxed me back by actually setting a wedding date. But now he's decided the upcoming date is just too soon – suddenly he thinks we have some problems that need ironing out first. But he can't really explain what they are.*

Whether he's a married man who promises to leave his wife as soon as she is emotionally able to handle their separation, an older man waiting for his mother to die or a younger man waiting for his career prospects to improve, anyone who continually begs for more time probably has taken up too much of yours already. He may be stringing you along until he meets Ms. Right or may simply be unable to make a decision. Don't let his excuses keep you tied up unless you are as unwilling to make a commitment as he is.

Some men, like Tony, are simply afraid of marriage and will eventually respond to an ultimatum. If his fear of losing you is greater than his fear of marriage, an impulsive wedding may be the best approach. Plunging ahead with an impulsive decision, such as rushing off to Gretna Green, may be the best way to deal with his fearful anticipation.

EDWARD: THE HOLDOUT

Sophie: *When we first met, Edward told me that I did not fit his picture of the woman he wanted to marry either intellectually or in terms of his personality. But we continued going out and had such a good time together that I assumed he had given up his fantasies and learned to appreciate my reality. Three years later, we're still going out and he still isn't sure he wants me.*

A self-respecting woman will not linger long in a relationship in which she is second best. Edward's Love Codes clearly suggest that Sophie is only a substitute for his fantasy woman. If he is too insecure or too intimidated to pursue the woman he really wants, he may ultimately ask Sophie to marry him, but he will never stop making negative comparisons. He may appreciate her desirable qualities but he will always feel cheated of passion and excitement. The result is certain to be a lack of intimacy; he may also grow increasingly critical and judgmental.

Caution: Men like Edward are prone to extramarital affairs because they feel they have been denied the opportunity to live out their fantasies. Although he may lack the self-confidence to leave an unsatisfactory relationship, the woman he marries may be stuck in a relationship based mostly on inertia and familiarity, not true love.

JOE: THE BIMBO SYNDROME

Suzanne: *Joe and I had a great first date and I was sure it was the beginning of something special, but he never called after that. Finally, I called him and he told me candidly that the woman he was looking to marry would be a blonde bombshell – and I just didn't qualify!*

Although they may go out with a range of women, a startling number of men seek out only classic beauties when the time comes to marry. These are men who have never overcome their own feelings of physical inferiority and think that a gorgeous woman will help them look good in the eyes of others. Ironically, should he be able to attract a genuine beauty, this man is capable of plunging into a relationship. However, even she will have to work hard to help him overcome his feelings of inadequacy. This man may never marry rather than settle for anything less than his ideal.

NICK: THE MARRYING KIND

Fiona: *Nick had been married three times but each marriage ended in an unhappy divorce. He complained that all three wives had faults that didn't surface until after the wedding day. I was sure things would be different between us, because I didn't have any of the faults that seemed particularly irritating to him. And his past history showed that at least he was eager to get married.*

A man who constantly finds fault with others actually has problems with his own self-image. If Fiona doesn't have the same faults as Nick's past wives, he is certain to find other reasons to criticise her. This man is the flip side of someone so afraid of intimacy that he never marries. Men like Nick are too insecure to be alone yet terrified of the vulnerability of marriage. Once they have a secure commitment, they tear away from it by incessant fault-finding and unreasonable criticism. Although a man's desire to get married may be an alluring attraction, it is unlikely that all three of his past wives were to blame.

ARE YOU COMPATIBLE?

If you want to avoid adding your relationship to the piles of false alarms out there, you had better find out just how compatible the two of you really are. The following questions will help you to unscramble his Love Codes and determine the long-term potential of this relationship.

Answer each question with Always, Frequently, Sometimes, Rarely, Never.

1. Does he have difficulty discussing his emotions?
2. Does he have difficulty understanding what you are telling him about your feelings?
3. Do trivial matters escalate into big disputes?
4. Does he look for excuses not to make love?
5. Have you discovered that he lies to you?
6. Are there times when you find that you've lost respect for him?
7. Does he engage in self-destructive behaviour, such as drinking, drugs or gambling?

8. Do you have heated arguments over political and religious issues?
9. Are you embarrassed to have him meet your friends and associates?
10. Does he tend to put you down or insult you?
11. Does he appear uninterested in your dreams and aspirations?
12. Will he pull away when you try to touch him?
13. Are you reluctant to tell him what you're really thinking?
14. Are the demands of his job more important to him than your needs?
15. Does he tend to blame you for his own failures and shortcomings?

The Score

Calculate his score with the following formula: Always = 0 points; Frequently = 1; Sometimes = 2; Rarely = 3; Never = 4. Add up his points, then read the revealing analysis that follows.

[49 – 60 points]
In every significant realm of your lives, you and this man are extraordinarily compatible. You have the ability to be perfectly open and frank with each other while maintaining a rich and satisfying romantic life. Generally you are in agreement about social and domestic issues and, if there are disputes, you have the maturity and resolve to settle them amicably. This man definitely has the potential to be a satisfying and loving partner.

[37 – 48 points]
Although you agree about many significant issues, there are a couple of key areas in which you do not see eye-to-eye. If you cannot find a point of compromise, it is important at

least to acknowledge your difference and agree to disagree. Overall, however, this man respects and understands you and is not afraid to show his affection. Although he can be a little moody at times, making you feel happy and secure is an important priority to him and he goes out of his way to do so.

[25 – 36 points]
This relationship has some real give-and-take to it. Although you share some important and satisfying areas of compatibility, your reservations about this man are justified. For now, it may be convenient to be with someone who is less than 100 per cent enamoured of you, because it provides the safety of keeping your options open. Are you ultimately destined to be together? Only time will tell, but the odds are that this relationship could become closer and more intimate if you are both willing to work at it.

[13 – 24 points]
Not much is cementing this union together. There are more areas of dispute than agreement and disturbingly little communication is taking place. Worse, you have reason to doubt his capacity ever to relate to you in the open and honest way that you would like. His self-centred tendencies make it difficult to reach him, even to discuss minor issues. Frankly, there's little chance of a growing, evolving relationship here.

[0 – 12 points]
Beware. Only pure masochism could be keeping this affair going, because the two of you have almost nothing in common. Every indicator suggests that if meaningful inter-action is your goal, then this man should be exorcised from your life as quickly as possible. To linger in a relationship as problem-ridden as this one is to admit to your own lack of self-worth. It is time for a hard look at the reasons why you feel entitled to so little.

WHY MEN FEAR INTIMACY

Fear of intimacy is the avoidance of deep emotional involvement with another person and it is the most common reason for a man to avoid marriage. Whether the origins of that fear are rooted in childhood experiences or in his relationship history, they suggest a deep-seated insecurity and a fear of being emotionally vulnerable.

Here is a look at the most common reasons that a man avoids intimacy – and what you can do about them.

She'll Leave Me

'I was in love once and when she broke up with me I was totally destroyed. I couldn't even go to work for a few weeks. I don't think I could live through that again and I certainly don't want to take the risk.'

This man fears that any woman he cares about will leave him, because he has not yet come to grips with the experiences of his past. Helping him take a hard look at the relationship that he lost might ease the pain of a past rejection and even make him realise the causes of the breakup. Most important, he can be helped to see that one rejection does not inevitably mean more will follow, especially if you can point out the difference between the past and the present.

She Won't Love Me When She Knows What I'm Really Like

'I know she thinks she's in love with me but that's because she doesn't really know me – only the confident, witty, charming exterior that I present. If she knows how insecure and frightened

I really am, she won't be interested. I'll never let her see that side of my personality, which is why I can't continue this relationship.'

Men continually underestimate women and misconstrue the source of their attraction to them. They don't realise that regardless of his public persona, most women do sense a man's insecurity and, within limits, they find it appealing. It helps to quell his insecurities if you let him know that you understand and appreciate him just the way he is.

She'll Betray My Trust

'Women say they want a man to share his feelings with them but they cannot be trusted. Eventually, out of hurt or anger, a woman will violate my trust and turn against me. I can't bear to be taunted about the confidences I shared with her in private.'

A woman who turns a man's confidences against him does indeed betray his trust. Even in the anger of the moment, it is a grave error to make hurtful accusations. A loyal and caring mate knows never to hit below the belt. A man's surest defence, however, is to accept his own failings; if he can do so, hearing them repeated by someone else will not be so devastating.

I'll Never Be Able To Satisfy Her

'I can't be the kind of man she wants me to be because I don't want to hear about her pain and frustrations, and I don't want to dwell on mine. I'd rather be her boyfriend, lover and playmate than her shrink or her saviour. I can't solve her problems with her family or make up for the love they didn't give her. I can only be me.'

Women put much more energy into a relationship than men do and expect a lot in return, although they often are unable to get it. The problem is that women traditionally believe that marriage is an intimacy based on shared feelings and emotional self-disclosure, whereas men seek an intimacy based on shared pleasures. If this relationship is to work both parties need to find a point of compromise that is reasonably satisfying to them both.

I'll Become Weak and Dependent

'Dawn made it too easy for me. She gave me too much too soon. She was generous in paying for dinners, theatre tickets and even holidays. She assumed the right to make all the decisions for both of us, and I began to feel overwhelmed – and smothered. Although it was certainly nice to be taken care of, I didn't like the loss of power that was involved.'

It is a fine line that a woman must toe in order to make a man feel comfortable and secure yet emotionally independent. Ironically, she achieves this by being responsive to him yet emotionally independent herself. Most men need to feel in control, even if the woman is really the aggressor, giving truth to the old saying that 'A man chases a woman until she catches him.'

Two exceptions to this premise: the man who was deprived of mothering as a child, or the one who craves the attention he once got from his mother, may be grateful for a wife who is willing to tend to his needs. Don't expect to shift roles after marriage, though – these men will always want to be smothered.

I'll Lose My Freedom And My Way Of Life

'Of course I get lonely sometimes but I'm not sure the benefits of marriage outweigh my reluctance to give you my freedom. Right now I feel like I have it all. A great flat, lots of friends and the excitement of meeting new women. I can work late or not at all, be a slob when I'm feeling lazy, and go out when I want to. I don't have to account for myself to anyone.'

In addition to leaving us the legacy of self-awareness and self indulgence, the 1960s ushered in a new attitude of flexibility in how relationships should be structured. The decade gave rise to a generation of men and women who fear the loss of freedom as much as they fear loneliness later in life. The struggle to establish a degree of independence within the framework of a committed relationship is a delicate process of negotiation, communication and compromise.

MAKING A COMMITMENT

How do you get a desirable man to overcome his fear of intimacy and commit to marriage? For many women, that is the million dollar question, and the key is to understand what most men are looking for in a wife. First and foremost, most men seek a woman with whom they feel secure and at ease. Shared goals, good sex, rewarding companionship, cosy intimacy, solace and pleasure are all important parts of deep-seated and lasting satisfaction. Although men are attracted to good-looking and intelligent women they often find glamorous and brilliant ones intimidating, an irony that highlights the extent to which most men are insecure.

It is no surprise, then, that men eventually choose to marry women with whom they feel intuitively comfortable. A woman, to secure a man's commitment, must make him feel desirable and safe; she must challenge him without overwhelming him. Other insights into a man's psyche are described in the following section.

What Men Really Want in a Woman

- Women develop feelings of intimacy much more quickly than men. Do not expect an intense response from him right away. Give him time to feel safe.
- A good sexual relationship holds the key to a man's heart, but he must feel as though he has been the aggressor. Although women equate satisfying sex with romance, men want to feel that you have succumbed to their charm, attractiveness, wit or intelligence. Although he will welcome your seductive gestures, he will not be comfortable if you take over.
- A man wants a woman who makes him feel special, not someone who worships him; he wants to be respected, not held in awe. The reason is clear: no man wants to

feel that he is the object of a woman's desperation. Men are attracted to popular women and like to think they have won her away from a horde of other suitors.

- Everybody needs to feel needed, and men go for women who are self-sufficient, yet love to be taken care of. Let him help you on with your coat, pay for dinner if he wishes and see you to the door: you'll be surprised at how much he appreciates the chance to show his courtesy.

- Assertive women are interesting and exciting; aggressive women are not. Men like women who are outgoing and take a certain amount of initiative, but they do not want to feel controlled or overwhelmed. Even the most passive man will be embarrassed if you are too bossy.

- Passive, overly accommodating women are wimpy and boring. Although a man may initially be attracted to a passive woman because she makes him feel safe and manly, he will lose respect for her and resent her lack of input.

- Men are turned on by a woman who reassures them, yet makes them feel they must work to win her over. This is a subtle art that requires you to be warm and caring when you're together but vaguely mysterious about your whereabouts at other times. Because they are trained to strive for achievement, a man values what he must work for more than what he receives without effort.

- A man likes to be with a woman who is his equal, but he is not interested in competing with her. Men look for women who can meet their emotional needs for warmth, support, nurturance and caring, not someone who insists on being one of the boys.

- A woman may make suggestions but not demands. Most men resist a woman who issues directives because she reminds him too much of his mother. Having asserted his independence once, he won't be eager to return again to a situation in which he feels like a child.

- In general, men need more space in relationships than women do. They value their autonomy and will feel suffocated by the degree of intimacy that most women seek. It is very important to maintain some independent interests of your own, because a man will not tolerate a woman who is addicted to his affection.

No matter how carefully you study his past history, analyse his personality and test your compatibility, intimate relationships pose challenges and often problems. Selecting the right mate is never an easy task. A man may look good at first, then reveal his true colours much later. Or he may be slow to open up, but prove steady and faithful once he learns to trust you.

Understanding the concept of Love Codes and learning to analyse them properly cuts way down on your chances of making a serious mistake. The point of this chapter, as it has been throughout the book, is to help you spot a man who is ready for a meaningful relationship – sometimes before he realises it himself. We believe that being part of a couple provides a warmth and joy that is unmatched in the human experience, and that once you are well-schooled in the art of Love Codes, finding the right mate is only a matter of time.

Happy hunting!